MANAGING
CONSTRUCTION CHANGES

**Managing Construction Changes:
Calculating the Cost**

Ben Wheeler, Texas

Copyright 2024, 2025 George P. Berg, PMP
ISBN 979-8-218-72310-1

MANAGING CONSTRUCTION CHANGES

Calculating the Cost

for Professional Builders
Second Edition

George P. Berg, PMP

Construction Research & Management Consulting

Table of Contents

Preface 7

Introduction 9

Contracts 13

Managing Changes 23

Getting Ahead of Conflicts 37

Early Warnings 43

Changes Happen 47

Calculating the Cost of Changes 69

Performance Measures 127

Conclusion 139

Daily Log Report 141

Acknowledgements 143

References 145

Preface

Construction contracts are designed to accommodate changes—that's what makes them unique among other types of contracts.

This book is intended for construction field supervisors, project engineers and project managers to better and more effectively manage construction projects and administer contracts.

In order to understand the contract, a discussion of general contracts—in easy-to-understand terms—is provided. Then, we'll provide suggestions for managing and pricing the cost of the inevitable—construction contract changes.

Demonstrating how changes affected a project, and the cost is difficult without a solid starting point.

Various methods are provided that were successfully used to calculate the cost of potential and actual inefficiencies and lost productivity on actual projects. Having a baseline (the "as planned") isn't always easy to establish. The bid, estimate, control budget and cost-loaded schedule are often different numbers as exact design and material prices fluctuate.

The source data used to illustrate the various effects of changes on construction projects has been around for decades. Many of the example calculations were used by the author and others to resolve complicated change orders and contract disputes. We will discuss ways to turn problems (e.g., bad weather, acceleration and other types of changes) into solutions.

The sample calculations demonstrate the magnitude, in time and money, of the profound impact changes can have on construction projects.

Finally, methods for making decisions in a structured, rational way are presented. With that, the following is offered to make construction and building projects a little less stressful and more rewarding for everyone involved.

This is NOT legal advice and should not be relied upon as a substitute for legal representation. It isn't legal counsel or a guarantee.

Introduction

Having the heart and soul of a builder and being involved in the construction industry has rewards probably found in only a few other occupations: enjoyment of the work in and of itself, the satisfaction of solving problems, the positive feelings of overcoming challenges, and providing for yourself and your family. Actually seeing, touching and even using a structure that you were part of creating can provide an extraordinary sense of satisfaction. A completed structure is something to point to with pride. We often hear and have said, "I built that…with my own hands."

Building is an ancient and honorable profession. After centuries, fundamental construction materials haven't changed all the much. We still use the combination of processed limestone, rock, gravel, sand and water (concrete), clay bricks, vitreous tile, steel (iron), glass made from silica sand, and wood from our forests. What we've added, among many other materials, are new and innovative composites that include plastics, fiberglass and micro-carbon fibers. Enhanced electronic equipment speeds up communication, making our ability to talk to our project partners faster.

However, talking to each other faster doesn't always solve problems. More often than not, it only describes them. Even with ConsensusDocs[1]* Contracts, Building Information Management (BIM) systems, Lean Construction, Value Engineering, Constructability Reviews and Partnering, construction projects

---

1   The ConsensusDocs are a series of contracts created by a construction community of designers, engineers, constructors, contractor associations, subcontractors and others to create a balanced and universally fair and equitable variety of construction and design contracts.

can quickly turn into trouble if the contractor doesn't read and understand the contract.

The hazards in building, if unmanaged, can be formidable. Construction is fast and often complicated, so staying out of trouble on building projects can be challenging. Avoiding trouble by preparing for it seems contradictory at first glance. It's not. Careful planning can be the difference between success and abject failure. The variables and unknowns (wildcards) inherent in construction present complex risks that can undue even an experienced builder armed with the most advanced technologies.

The financial risks on construction projects can be hidden in the estimating, bidding and budgeting process. Portions of the estimate can be underestimated or the entire job underpriced. More often than we like, price contingences are eliminated. The buyout and preparing the bill of materials can include surprises when quotes offered by vendors turn out to be an order of magnitude—just a guess by a salesman. Getting signed subcontracts and sorting through the various vendors' offers presents a variety of issues—the temptation to shop bids to get the best deal is there. Occasionally, contractors start work without a signed contract.

Frequently, the wild card is labor: inadequate skill sets or not enough of the "good ones." The availability of competent foremen and need to rely on underqualified field managers are perennial industry challenges. Various languages spoken on job sites can be confusing as direction can be lost in translation. Design dimensions in metric must be converted into feet and inches so they make sense in the field.

Budget constraints, time limits, owners, architects, engineers and more all play a role. "Bad plans" is the catchall phrase used by contractors to describe what was given to them by the designers to build the project. Inspectors can over-inspect and demand a degree of compliance or performance for items not in the contract. Unanticipated changes in the weather, site conditions and unmarked underground utilities can slow down or even delay construction. The user group that is going to occupy the facility (when it's complete or even when it's not complete) often enjoys touring the job site and suggesting changes—coffee cups in hand, expecting their ideas to be miraculously incorporated. Even grumpy neighbors and adjacent landowners can affect the success of projects.

Staying out of trouble by preventing (or mitigating) trouble before it happens allows contractors to stay in business. Knowing how to price the inevitable changes and use the contract to your advantage might (might) keep you and the entire team out of trouble.

Preventing by preparing is unquestionably the best way to handle potential trouble by avoiding it altogether.

Chapter 1

Contracts

Much has been written about construction contracts. Universities, law libraries and the heads of legal scholars are filled with the theory of the law regarding contracts and specifically construction contracts. Construction law is more than just the law applied to the business of building.

Contracts are necessary in building and construction. They are a tool and should be used like one. Contracts can invoke a sort of disdain, some mystery and the "awe shucks by golly" nostalgia for the good old days. Those "good ole' days" of doing business on a handshake may never have really existed anyway. We've always had contracts. Contracts for construction were used in the early-American colonial days and were basically the same as they are today. What has changed is the amount of detail and the technical specifications.

Owners, architects, engineers, general contractors, subcontractors, inspectors, vendors and suppliers have different perspectives and perceptions. Fifty or more companies may share a construction job site. What holds these very different groups with divergent interests together is "the law between the parties"—the contracts. Good faith and trusting souls notwithstanding, without contracts there would be chaos and very little, if anything, would get done.

Interpreting the "law between parties" (the contract) is aided by years of resolving past problems decided by judges and juries. Clearly, there is history for resolving "who done it" when there is a dispute on a construction project. The heavy lifting has been finished, and many decisions have already been made.

What remains is discovering the specific facts related to the particular project and the cause of the trouble. Deciding how much and who is responsible to pay for changes are the challenge. Those who decide the outcome will be guided by previous resolutions but, more importantly, the facts of the current dispute.

In order to resolve potential trouble before people get upset and attorneys get involved, there must be a clear set of facts in the project record. The project record is the documentation of everything that happens during a specific project (ie. material deliveries, weather delays, change requests, etc.).

That starts by clearly understanding the basic components of the contract.

The key to resolving or minimizing problems is to know when, where and why things changed from the original plan. For the project team to be able to do this, they must clearly understand the basic terms and conditions of the contract and the scope of work it defines.

To become more comfortable reading contracts and sharing the terms and conditions with your teams, we should start at the beginning.

Contract Defined

There are a variety of ways to define a contract. All of them return to the law for their authority.

Barron's Law Dictionary definition: A promise, for the breach of which the law provides a remedy, or performance of which the law recognizes a duty.

The U.S. Uniform Commercial Code: The total obligation in law which results from the party's agreement as affected by this Act and any other applicable rules or laws.

Corbin on Contracts by Arthur Corbin, etal.: Every agreement and promise enforceable by law is a contract.

To make it a binding contract, the following basic components must be considered:

- Offer

- Acceptance
- Consideration
- Enforceability requirements
- Legal purpose
- Age of majority
- Control of mental capacity

Contract Rules of Interpretation

Rule 1: Reasonable, Logical Interpretation.

Rule 2: Manifest Intent of Drafter. One of the important interpretation "aids" to be considered is the intention of the drafter of the contract—as manifested by the words, phrases, symbols or legends they elected to use.

Rule 3: Look to the Whole Agreement of the Contract. Of all the "aids" to reasonable interpretation, none is used more frequently than the "whole agreement" rule, i.e. "we will look within the four corners of the contract to determine its meaning." No one section will be read alone in such a manner to make it inconsistent and defeat the uniform purpose of all the sections interpreted as a whole.

Rule 4: Normal Meaning of Words. Words, symbols and marks will be given their common and normal meaning, unless it is clearly shown that such words, symbols or marks have:

- Either a technical meaning and were used in the contract in their technical sense, or
- Some other special meaning accorded to them by the parties.

Rule 5: The Principal and Apparent Purpose of the Contract. Illogical Interpretation or Interpretations that lead to absurdity will be disregarded. One of the maxims of interpretation to be "given great weight" in ascertaining a contract's reasonable meaning is the principal apparent purpose of the contract.

Rule 6: Custom and Usage. Words are given meaning as the trade involved understands them. Custom and usage of the trade is commonly used as an "aid" to interpretation in two situations:

- Where it is necessary to add a term to the contract without which the obligations of one or both of the parties would be unclear;
- Where a custom and usage is needed to clarify an otherwise ambiguous provision.

Rule 7: Knowledge of Other Party's Interpretation. This rule, that a contracting party is bound by his knowledge of the other party's interpretation unless he indicates disagreement, is steeped in ethics as well as law. It is based on the principle that an interpretation is unreasonable if it permits one contracting party to take advantage of another. The provisions of the contract should be interpreted as they were understood by the parties (including all contractors) before the dispute arose.

Rule 8: Concurrent Interpretation. Where there is evidence of a concurrent interpretation by:

- Other bidders prior to entering the contract, or
- The parties or their representatives during performance and before a controversy arises, or
- The subcontractors before a controversy arises. Such an interpretation (unless clearly erroneous) is given great, if not controlling, weight.

Rule 9: Order of Precedence. Contracts frequently set forth the precedence to be accorded to words, terms and drawings should it develop that conflict exists between them. For example, general specifications take precedence over drawings, specific provisions over general provisions, implied provisions and printed provisions.

Rule 10: Construed Against Drafter. If the words are ambiguous, the provision will be construed against the party who drafted it. This rule is known as the doctrine of "contra proferentem." Ambiguities, which form the basis of many disputes, are generally construed against the owner.

Rule 11: Parol Evidence. The parol provides that, where two parties have reduced their agreement to a written contract, all prior negotiations and understandings (whether written or oral) are merged into the contract and cannot be used to contradict the express terms of the contract.

Rule 12: Duty to Seek Clarification. When ambiguity is obvious or patent, a party has an obligation to seek clarification. However, lack of strict compliance with the timely notice provision need not be fatal to your position.

Contract Administration v. Project Management

Are contract administrators and project managers the same? The answer is, of course, yes and no. The complication is that, on occasion, they are the same person.

The project manager is responsible for project completion: doing it safely, with the quality defined in the contract documents, on time and within a budget. Ultimately it's the job of the project manager to finish the project and bring it online. How that gets done is discretionary.

The role of the contract administrator is similar to the role of a project manager, related but not the same. The contract administrator is concerned with enforcing the terms and conditions of the contract. They may be fair and reasonable but the emphasis, in fact the purpose of contract administration is compliance with the terms and conditions of the contract.

Here's one way to look at the differences:

Contract Administrator	Project Manager
Enforce administrative procedures	"Horse trade" and make deals
Compliance	Get results
Corporate orientation	Project oriented
"Get it in writing"	Field expediency
According to specifications	Done right, within budget

Contract Administrator	Project Manager
Strict adherence to contract documents	"Work out" problems in the field; minimize paperwork

The differences are more about how rather than what. Both the project manager and contract administrator will get the job done; it's just a matter of emphasis. This balancing act requires judgment, maturity and experience.

There can be contradictions in the roles of a project manager and contract administrator, which can be exacerbated when the same person performs both these responsibilities.

Both roles include but are not limited to:

- Technical supervision
- Change order issuance and negotiation
- Dispute review, settlement and disposition
- Price analysis and negotiation
- Inspection and acceptance
- Manage Quality, Schedule and Cost (probably in that order)

Personnel on the Project

A lot of people and organizations influence the construction outcome with varying degrees of authority or lack of authority on a project. The actual authority of all the players throughout the life of the project must be clearly established and followed from the start of the contract.

Construction contracts can be written so that only the owner can authorize change orders that increase the contract price. The design professional may be limited to authorizing minor changes that do not affect the price. Federal government contracts typically state that only the CO, or his authorized representative, has authority to issue orders requiring contractors to perform changes or extra work.

Personnel Working for the Owner

Know whom you're dealing with. The principle rule regarding personnel working for the owner and contracts is that the owner will not consider themselves bound by the unauthorized acts of employees. Contractors must understand the legal authority of the individual with whom we are dealing. Relying on someone's apparent authority is not an excuse if things go wrong.

Delegation of Authorities

As contractors we must understand the limits and authority of the people on the project. Contracting authority is generally granted via formal delegation by the head of a procuring organization (owner). On some state and federal projects, delegation is required to be prominently displayed in the field office of the owner's representative by issuance of a Certificate of Appointment. This appointment describes those individuals with authority to execute and interpret contractual documents that can bind the owner. This authority includes, but is not limited to, the execution, termination and changing of contract requirements.

Authorized Representatives

Figure out who is or are the owner's representatives(s). Generally, authorized representatives are appointed in writing with their authority specified at contract inception. They are the eyes and ears of the owner but usually cannot authorize change. Delegated authority can refer to one or more contracts, with the general exception that the authorized representative may not modify a contract. In a few instances, the owner may delegate various types of authority, with the written understanding that any direction given to a contractor must not involve changes in the price, the quantity, the quality or the delivery schedule of the contract. If it isn't clear—ask.

Contractors must be extremely aware with whom they are dealing and their legal and actual authority. If the person who "suggests" a change does not have the contractual or legal authority to bind the owner (no matter how hard they try to convince you), the contractor may not be paid for the change. The majority of the personnel you deal with daily won't have authority.

Ratification Procedures - Unauthorized Authority

Know all the players. Ratification is the performed work that was originally demanded by someone without authority, but the owner later agrees to. However, it must be clearly understood that ratification cannot occur unless the owner has benefited and received something of value. It is critical that the complete and total text of the contract—all the terms and conditions—be reviewed and understood to avoid ratification.

Imputed Knowledge/Authorized Personnel

In construction contracts, it's critical to understand the importance of whether or not the owner has knowledge of certain facts (and didn't tell anyone) that may later become the subject of a change order request or a contract dispute. Specifically, such knowledge may be important because of the notice requirements in the contract and its relationship to the various entitlement provisions, i.e., changes clause, suspension of work clause, termination for convenience, damages for delay, time extension, etc. Additionally, the owner may accept the responsibility that the information known by an inspector or representative becomes the owner's.

Technical Representatives

In general, the technical representative, e.g. architect or engineer hired by owner, functions with limited authority with regard to contract changes. However, in the area of imputed knowledge and the representative's responsibility to deliver critical information to the owner, it's generally accepted that the owner utilizes their technical representatives as their "eyes and ears," and their knowledge is treated, for all intents and purposes, as the owner's. It's assumed that if the design team knows something, the owner also knows the same thing.

Inspectors

Contractors are generally well aware that on-site inspectors do not have the same designated authority as technical representatives of the owner. Inspectors clearly are not authorized to make changes to the contract terms and conditions, specification, drawings or schedule. There should always be the presumption that an inspector is not an authorized representative. Therefore, changes to the work based upon an inspector's direction or suggestion that have a cost impact (either adding or deleting work) to the contract will normally be at the contractor's risk and liability. Inspectors may overstep their authority and demand work not in the contract.

Bottomline, contractors are responsible for compliance with the terms and conditions of the contract and for understanding the full authority of the owner personnel with whom they operate on a daily basis. Contractors must clearly understand their responsibilities. Failure to do so is not a reason for compensation for any costs or problems associated with taking direction from an unauthorized person or representative.

Chapter 2

Managing Changes

Compared to other business agreements, construction contracts are unique in that they have a built-in mechanism for changes that will inevitably occur: the changes clause. To settle trouble and disagreements, learn to use the changes clause found in almost all well-written construction contracts.

Frequently, change orders (Equitable Adjustment Requests in federal government work) involve instructions or directives from the owner or the design professional. It's imperative to act on such instructions only when the particular representative has actual authority to issue orders (see Chapter 1). If the representative lacks authority and the work is carried out, payment may be denied.

Contractors may be placed in a position that appears to be opposite an owner, with the goal to complete the project with the quality defined by the contract, on time, and hopefully make a profit while not making anyone angry.

The owner's goal is usually to complete the project as quickly as possible, maintain quality and hold costs to a minimum. The inherent nature of these two objectives seems to be diametrically opposed. Few projects ever run their cycle without changes and fewer still are completed without leaving some element of quality, schedule or cost unresolved. Projects can end imperfectly with no one completely satisfied with the outcome.

The contract must be read with a particular focus on the changes clause, the notice provisions and the technical specifications at a minimum.

Only reasonable change orders should be pursued. Being trigger-happy or a "claim jumper" who initiates a change on every matter that arises during performance exercises judgment as poor as that of the manager who believes it is good business to "get along" by never filing a change order. It's wise to request only those change orders that are of sufficient size and merit to warrant the preparation necessary for successful settlement.

Filing inconsequential or unmeritorious requests for extra money tends to cause even more trouble and discredit you, the company, and the request.

Change Clauses

Changes, or work beyond contract requirements, can take forms not readily apparent. Various clauses within the contract spell out how to recoup payment. A change order submitted after final payment is not allowed ("a stale claim"), so it's important to take care of as they arise. Owners may resist the issuance of a change order; however, if work is required beyond that specified in the contract, change orders apply.

Constructive change is when defective specifications require rework or modification of work already completed. It can also result from instructions or contract interpretations rendered by a design professional or, in the case of federal government contracts, the contracting officer (CO). Often a design professional will believe their instructions or interpretation does nothing more than restate what was originally required by the contract, while in fact, such directives require significantly more or a different type of work.

Changed conditions or differing site conditions clause are used when unanticipated subsurface or other site conditions results in extra work. Conduct a site investigation after bid as well as prebid and bring any potential site condition concerns, obvious relocation problems or access issues to the attention of the owner.

Because of the frequencies of such conditions, many construction contracts have this clause built in. Such a clause obviously benefits contractors, but in the long run, it also saves the owner money by allowing the elimination of some contingency costs from the bid. Such clauses are usually standard in federal government contracts.

The presence of a differing site conditions clause saves the trouble of using the argument of the implied warranty of plans and specifications—the alternative when the contract lacks such a provision. However, when the differing site conditions clause is present, reimbursement for that extra cost may be waived if the existence of the condition is not immediately recognized and appropriate notice not given to the owner.

Naturally, site conditions different from those represented in the contract cannot be recognized unless project personnel are intimately familiar with prebid site conditions and contract scope of work. This understanding of the contract allows expectations to be measured against what is actually experienced during construction.

Constructive acceleration comes into play when the contractor is entitled to a time extension because the owner suspends or delays work, but a time extension is totally or partially denied by the owner's representative.

It can also be used when the owner threatens to impose liquidated damages and forces a contractor to accelerate the pace of the work by adding additional workers or equipment, or by shifting existing crews to overtime schedules without asserting any contract rights. Acceleration increases direct costs and frequently generates inefficiencies. If a contractor is entitled to an extension of time, both direct and indirect costs attributable to the acceleration costs should be paid.

Delays and disruption, companions to acceleration discussed previously, may result from the owner's acts or failure to act. To recognize when this clause applies, a working knowledge of the construction schedule and its relationship to the owner's actions is required. Such knowledge ensures appropriate notices can be given and information preserved. Unwarranted work rejection or over inspection provides a basis for a change order if site personnel recognize the condition in sufficient time to provide the required notices and maintain supporting documentation.

Notice Provisions

Construction contracts normally provide that change orders may not be requested unless written notice is received by the owner or its representative within a specified period of time. For example, the American Institute of Architects (AIA) Standard General Contract Form (AIA Document A201 1976 ed.) contains a number of notice requirements. Although many of the time limits are twenty (20) days—they can be different.

The ConsensusDoc 200 contract documents require:

8.4 CHANGES NOTICE Except as provided in 6.3.2 and 6.4 (referring to previous articles) for any claim for an increase in the Contract Price and or Contract Time, Constructor shall give owner written notice of the claim within fourteen (14) Days after the occurrence giving rise to the claim or within fourteen (14) Days after Constructor first recognizes the condition giving rise to the claim, whichever is later.

Additionally, Constructors can have a limited time within which to submit proof of their claims. For example, in ConsensusDocs article 8.4 it says:

Therefore, Constructor shall submit written documentation of its claim, including appropriate supporting documentation, within twenty-one (21) Days after giving notice, unless the Parties mutually agree upon a longer period of time.

The phrase *time is of the essence* has significant meaning and is included in many contracts. Essentially that means all time limits stated in the contract are important, and trouble is imminent if they are ignored or brushed off. The ConsensusDocs family of contracts have provisions with multiple time limits of thirty (30), fifteen (15) and seven (7) days for various articles besides the fourteen (14) and twenty-one (21) days for changes. All of them have an element of "time is of the essence."

Government construction contracts provide that change orders may generally not be presented unless written notice is given to the government within certain specified time limits.

"Men must turn square corners when they deal with the government," Rock Island, Arkansas & Louisiana R.R. Co vs United States, 254 U.S. 141, 143 (1920).

The following are examples of notice requirements in the government contracts. When a government contractor believes it has encountered a "constructive change," the contractor must, in accordance with Federal Acquisition Regulations (FAR) 52.2403-4:

Provide notice of a claim (except in the case of defective specifications) within twenty (20) days after the occurrence of the constructive change. Constructive change costs incurred more than twenty (20) days before written notice to the CO will probably not be considered for payment. In addition, either along with the above notice, or thirty (30) days thereafter, submit a written statement of the general nature and financial scope of the constructive changes assertion (although the Government may extend the thirty (30) day period).

The "Differing Site Conditions" clause for construction contracts (sometimes called the "changed conditions" clause) requires Contractors to notify the CO of any differing site conditions "promptly, and before such conditions are disturbed." Otherwise any claim based on such conditions may be denied. The "Suspension of Work" clause for construction contracts provides that suspension costs incurred more than twenty (20) days before a Contractor gives the CO written notice of circumstances which regarded as suspension are not going to be reimbursed (except that such a notice need not be given if the suspension resulted from an actual suspension order by the CO). In addition, a change order request (including the amount) must in all cases be in writing. Compliance with these notice requirements is essential. Time is of the essence.

The right to payment has more support if the owner or CO knew of the change and (by silence or acquiescence) ratified it. The safest course when receiving instructions from a representative, who may not have the authority to order extra work, is to write the owner, reporting the instruction stating that if required to perform the work—a change order request will be submitted. The owner then has a fair opportunity to:

- Direct that the work not be performed (in which case there is no further problem)
- Ratify the representative's instructions
- By silence and failure to repudiate them, show acquiescence in the instructions. Silence is ascension—agreement.

If the owner ratifies or acquiesces the instructions, they become in effect "owned" and the right to additional compensation and time extensions is preserved. Writing a confirmation letter is not only reasonable but should be appreciated by the owner, since it avoids misunderstanding before the work is performed.

Written confirmation from the owner or design professional should be obtained for all oral instructions and directives, even when the contract does not specifically require it. This avoids trouble regarding the scope of the instructions. It alerts the design professional to a particular directive issued by its agents or representatives. It also provides the owner with an opportunity to clarify, define or rescind the directive before costs are incurred. If a design professional refuses to confirm oral instructions in writing, confirm the instructions by letter to that design professional, with a copy to the owner.

Technical Specifications

Field managers should be aware of events and conditions associated with the contract so that resolution can happen prior to completion of the changed work and, more importantly, have the cost of the additional work agreed upon before it is completed. Field managers must be proactive to stay out of trouble and take care of business. By knowing what is in the agreement ("the deal"), the field manager will be:

- More able to comply with procedural requirements
- Likely to have adequate records of costs for the potential issue which produced the need for a change order request
- Quick to recognize the need to document circumstances or details of events
- More likely to get paid while doing the extra work

Avoid volunteering and performing work outside the scope of the contract without first documenting it in writing and adding a Reservation of Rights for future costs as yet unknown or knowable. Notifying the owner of the intent to evaluate the impact and submit pricing data at such time as it may be reasonable to determine the costs of the increased work effort. Providing notice by email, text or other electronic means that cannot be altered or erased can be discussed at any of the initial project team meetings.

Again, to avoid complications associated with changes and be able to present solutions to potential project problems, the construction team should be familiar with:

- Specific drawings and specifications references
- Correct performance of all contract requirements
- Open Requests For Information (RFIs), submittals, addenda, etc.
- Accurate recordkeeping and correspondence
- Thorough presentation preparation
- Facts supporting the issues
- Proposed schedule modifications
- Estimates based on industry standards and their own business financial records
- Administrative controls and traceability

Tracking Work

Very often it's part of the field manager's job to ensure there is a clear set of facts about what occurred or is occurring in the project record (i.e. the paperwork). These records should be WRITTEN and, where appropriate, photographed. There's an old saying heard in medicine and in the military: "If it's not written down, it didn't happen."

If it's not written down, it didn't happen.

Document System

Contractors have a tendency to approach each new job optimistically, assuming that it can be timely and profitably completed without trouble, but this isn't always the case. Instead of relying on blind optimism, utilizing a project documentation system serves two important functions:

- Ensures adequate control and monitoring of the project.
- Creates an accurate and complete record of job conditions and potential problems and their impact on the project.

While it may be somewhat unpleasant to begin a project with an eye to possible future trouble, the failure to adopt such prudent management procedures almost inevitably ensures that problems will develop.

Documenting the many complicated problems which arise during the course of construction is burdensome for job site personnel charged with that responsibility. Nevertheless, since documentation almost invariably determines success, the importance of building the record cannot be overemphasized.

We've been reminded of the expression, "The money is in the paper."

Records

Contractors may discover that their change requests are subject to technical troubles because they have not kept a step-by-step record of what occurred or is occurring.

Among the most encountered records valuable for good project management, the avoidance of trouble and argument resolution are:

- Project correspondence
- Meeting minutes
- Job site logs (i.e. RFIs, Submittals, addenda, etc.)
- Conversation memos
- Photographs
- Job cost accounting records
- Contract notices and correspondence

Project Correspondence

The phrase included in construction contracts "time is of the essence" means "hurry up every chance you get" when reporting project problems. Correspondence should be simple, factual and brief. Describe the problem, state the recommended solution and request additional time and money for the contract change. Timely notice must be issued immediately upon discovering the problem area.

An overreliance on the fallible memories of team members with competing interests is always a bad idea. Often the root cause of trouble is distorted memories of what people think actually happened on a project.

Meeting Minutes

Detailed and accurate meeting minutes help avoid future trouble and can support potential change orders. The minutes should be completed immediately after each meeting and distributed to all individuals who attended the meeting. Minutes should be prepared in complete detail and verified against the notes of all other individuals in the organization who attended.

Documentation of directives obtained during a meeting can save problems later. Always prepare (or suggest) and distribute an agenda prior to the meeting so attendees can come prepared.

A recording device, camera or a video recorder can be used (with permission) during a meeting to provide absolute, undeniable documentation and often will improve the quality of the meetings themselves.

Job Site Logs

The ideal job site log is one that provides a daily record of work progress together with periodic summaries of conditions at the site. To the extent that the log performs these functions, it can be a major factor settling arguments about what happened.

Such contemporaneous written records of site conditions and any record of a contractual "hurt" can also provide valuable facts down the road. The obvious inference from good, accurate records is that the one who protested loudly at the time of an alleged injury sustained it.

The status of open RFIs, submittals and change orders, pricing information, and contract accounting can be determined immediately from accurate and up-to-date project logs. Keeping logs for potential (pending) problems or an event that might become a change order can be made part the "early warning" management system.

All staff must be aware of the importance and value of accurate and thorough documentation. Without it, the impact of weather conditions, delays, and acceleration can jeopardize the project and their own paychecks. Field personnel, in particular, are often reluctant to properly and adequately report site conditions regularly. Personnel at all levels within the organization should stay aware of the importance of documentation and should be encouraged to overdocument if necessary. It's not possible to have too much information of actual conditions.

One of the great advantages of a log maintained on a daily basis is that it provides observations and evaluations by personnel in the form of a regular business record. Upper management will readily appreciate the value of a "regularly kept business record." If and when the matter must be negotiated, regularly kept business records might be admissible as an exception to the hearsay rule.

Senior managers should encourage their team members to maintain such a daily recording system from the beginning of a project, although it becomes particularly crucial with the onset of problems. One means of helping the project team keep a detailed daily record is to use a voice recording device. This makes it convenient to record notes and observations during job site trailer time or at the end of the day. This recording can be returned for word processing to the home office where a central log is maintained and a copy returned to the job site.

Managers can further encourage comprehensive reports by supplying the superintendent with a template or outline. The outline should lay out the categories the superintendent should comment on each workday.

It's important that the person responsible for the log be reminded of the importance of recording everything pertinent to the most common types of problems. If, for example, the field manager fails to record circumstances for a delay or extra work, the very fact that nothing was included in the report may make it look like no such delay or extra work actually occurred.

An outline for dictation should at least include:

- A description of the weather conditions
- A description of the work performed
- A list of the materials delivered to the site
- Other potential issues

See Addendum for a sample daily log you can copy and use.

Conversation Memos

Contemporaneous memos of project conferences and conversations with the owner, the architect, engineer, inspector, subcontractors and suppliers can be valuable months or years later in reconstructing the substance of those meetings. Reference to such conferences should be made in the job site record where they include the field managers or job superintendent.

An even better approach, where appropriate, is a prompt letter sent to the other parties who were present, summarizing the substance of the conversation or meeting. This gives the other party an opportunity to object if there's a dispute over interpretation of what actually took place.

Photographs

No project of any size can afford to be without a camera or video. Digital is preferable because it allows the party responsible for picture taking to check the content and clarity of photos while still at the site and before conditions are altered. Sometimes a professional photographer or videographer may be needed, but generally job site personnel are adequate. Phone photographs are valuable if they can be transferred and/or printed for the record.

The ideal approach to picture taking is to view photographs as a diary of the job. This encourages personnel to take photographs of site conditions on a routine and systematic basis, perhaps concentrating on problem areas and those areas associated with crucial construction procedures and scheduling. Printed photographs should be identified on the back with a notation as to time, date, location, conditions depicted, persons present and the photographer.

A particularly effective use of photography is a panoramic photo showing large portions of the site. No special equipment is necessary. This can be achieved by taking separate photos at intervals on a 180-degree arc. These photos can then be matched and viewed together to give a more realistic feel for the relationship of various areas and activities on the work site.

> *One picture is worth a thousand words.*

Everyone is acquainted with the expression "one picture is worth a thousand words." For contractors, one picture can be worth thousands of dollars. Indeed, photographs can, in some cases, be more useful than personnel's memories when conditions are difficult to describe.

Photographs are also useful for educating and persuading others about construction techniques and problems, as well as preserving facts regarding conditions which may be covered by later work.

Job Cost Accounting Records

The use of effective accounting methods and the maintenance of appropriate cost records can minimize many of the proof problems inherently associated with construction contracts. Proving the actual dollars lost is particularly true with government contracts where Government Accounting Office (GAO) standards are more stringent. The same strict standards can be found in private, state and local contracts.

The need for a method of isolating costs not covered by the contract is especially prevalent during delay, acceleration and impact changes, since these frequently involve inefficiency and loss of productivity which are difficult to break out under a more traditional accounting system. A system, which allows for segregation of unanticipated costs, is not only easier and less expensive than an after-the-fact breakdown, it's more convincing. Keep track of the costs of changes separately for labor, equipment, materials and subcontracts.

Scheduling programs such as short interval schedules, bar charts and the CPM can be used to illustrate delays and disruptions and their impact on the project. Scheduling programs can also include job costs for individual activities. For this reason, if CPM scheduling is justified by the size of the project, coordination between the scheduling and cost accounting systems is a key to being consistent and not contradictory.

Track the costs of extra work to the cause of the change as precisely as possible. Classically, identify problems and releases (e.g. lien releases) during performance, before they have been etched in granite.

The process of establishing the validity of the change order must be distinguished from the process of identifying the change order itself.

Contract Notices and Coordination

Again, the success of a change order depends on proving that notice, sufficient to satisfy the requirements of the contract, was provided to the owner or their representative. The entire construction team needs to be thoroughly familiar with all provisions of the contract, but especially with those relating to notice, particularly in standardized contracts, where what constitutes "adequate" notice is very clear.

Failure to give appropriate notice or to retain a copy of a notice that is sent may doom a change request for reimbursement for extra work or delay in the schedule. It may also force a long, drawn-out and expensive negotiation to prove waiver, modification or actual knowledge. All correspondence, even notes and memos jotted on scraps of paper, should be preserved. These may be the key to proving waiver or modification of the contract.

Identifying Areas for Change Orders

Getting prepared to submit a change order starts with determining why the project is losing money or falling behind schedule. The next logical step is to see if there is a contract change provision that addresses the issues. Many contractors sign contracts with the intent of not requesting changes because they assume there won't be any.

Therefore their job cost records do not alert them to losses when there are construction changes.

Often contractors look backward at the losses that have already occurred. This book should teach you to keep good records along the way and get ahead of any changes that need to be made.

In addition, there may be situations where the losses aren't readily recognizable. For example, an existing defective specification is a basis for a valid change request but with inadequate contract controls, it's not easy to figure out. In such a situation, there should be an extra check, specifically cost control procedures which are believable and will give an early warning of the possibility of trouble, e.g., lower productivity than planned.

Chapter 3

Getting Ahead of Conflicts

Upper management should, at the outset of a project, determine the extent to which facts are being preserved and encourage the project personnel to revise unsatisfactory procedures. For example, whenever a subcontractor is terminated or defaults, the prime contractor should, as a matter of routine, immediately order a survey or work-in-place. Such a survey simplifies settlements with and claims against a bonded subcontractor's surety for the cost of completion. It may, in some instances, prevent the surety from raising overpayment as a defense to payment on the sub's bond and eliminate any disconnect about the quantity and quality of work in place. The survey will similarly facilitate claims against a solvent unbonded (without a bond) subcontractor.

Such documentation also benefits both the owner and the general contractor because it can prevent disputes between these parties. By initiating a survey of work in place, a prime contractor may protect against an action that terminates the prime for "excessive costs to complete" brought by an owner that might stick the prime contractor with the cost.

Contract provisions can generally be found, within certain limitations, to support the positions of both parties. Therefore, persuasive presentation of facts is the key to getting approval on a disputed change order, and it is in the presentation and interpretation of these facts where the team may need help.

Bringing in Experts

As a rule, it's wise to involve a range of experienced professionals throughout construction. If problems appear early in the project, these experts may suggest ways of mitigating damages or reducing the impact. They also may be able to recommend methods of preserving facts for use during negotiation and arbitration.

On fast-moving, complex construction projects, the services of a variety of experts may be required. For example, subsurface problems frequently require a soils engineer or hydrologist, while rock problems necessitate the services of a geological expert. Structural engineers may be needed to determine the causes of problems plaguing construction of the building itself.

Scheduling experts can help deal with the effects of delay, disruption and acceleration. Frequently, contracts will require retaining the services of a scheduling engineer for developing and updating a CPM or similar schedule.

The legal department or an attorney is another expert whose involvement is desirable when problems begin to develop. Construction attorneys are frequently knowledgeable in specialized areas such as accounting and scheduling. If they lack the expertise, they might know experts whose services could benefit the project.

Finally, senior managers regularly communicating with the team during construction will acquire firsthand knowledge of any problems. This knowledge will then make their help in negotiation more persuasive than if it were based solely on facts learned from others.

Detailed records of time and cost increases, photographs, videos, correspondence and memos relative to the individual problem can be kept and maintained in separate "issue files." Almost anything written—data entry, original documents, inspection reports, meeting notes, receipts, and timecards—are historical documents that must track consistently and not contradict one another. The quantity and quality of this documentation will substantially affect the odds of success during negotiation.

When managed efficiently, a documentation system is an invaluable supervisory and monitoring tool for any given project. Data is used to plan and control each phase of the operation. The history of the project provides the essential data to document, or in the worst case, you can use it to diagnose what went wrong to avoid making the same mistake in the future.

Reputations as a professional construction company or as a well-regarded manager are won and lost because of adequate documentation. The interests of construction companies can be protected with systematic, consistent record keeping of the project's progress. The following is a summary of documents (a minimum) that should be maintained:

- Site investigation report
- Project correspondence
- Daily report
- Change order, RFIs, Addenda logs
- Meeting minutes
- Photographs

The site investigation report (what the estimators saw or read) is the first documentation of the project. Critically important support for resolving controversial issues can be obtained from a properly written site investigation report. The report describes the conditions of the project prior to bid and establishes an understanding of the project itself.

An "as-bid" condition is established by the site investigation report and transforms into documentation of "as-bid" conditions as the project progresses.

Prior to the actual bid, establish exactly what information is recorded on the site investigation report. The company's report form can be modified as experience with different project types is obtained and revisions noted.

Timely Notice

When there is a breakdown in communication, owner-caused problems are likely. The first and most critical step is giving timely notice. Providing notice is not necessarily an easy task. Giving notice the wrong way can be seen as aggressive, akin to firing the first shot at the owner.

A phone call by the contractor's project manager to the appropriate team member might help remind the team that notice is a contractual obligation that benefits everyone. Prior to sending a "nasty gram," make a phone call explaining to the owner that they will be getting a letter (email or text) regarding the particular issue. This professional courtesy might keep the owner from feeling blindsided.

Correspondence should be simple, as immediate identification is critical. A letter (text or email if agreed upon at the outset) should be concise, including the location, date, time, and citing references, drawings and specifications if applicable. Wherever possible, estimate the potential time and approximate cost increases which will or may be caused by the problem, and establish the company's position on how the problem should be resolved. State your intentions in dealing with the problem (ie. "work is on hold") and request resolution by a specific date. Timing is everything. The tone should be professional, business-like, dispassionate, but still pleasant.

When explaining additional costs to the owner, be sure to include a "reservation of right" comment or sentence. This will enable adding impact costs when they can be identified and calculated. Analyze the contract's terms and request clarification on any ambiguous language.

Many contracts contain a time limit in the notice provision— check the contract. The specified times may vary, and the wording occurs in endless varieties, but the intent is always very clear: the contractor must give written notice.

The notice requirement is logical, legitimate, and in most cases, enforceable. The owner enjoys the right to mitigate the additional costs of a change order. For example, a $1,000 design effort might eliminate a $10,000 construction change. Therefore, we have an absolute duty to give timely notice so the owner can exercise their right to eliminate or mitigate a problem. Many contract disputes have been decided against contractors who failed to comply with the written notice provision.

Constructive Notice

If the owner knew, or should have known, about the problem via onsite knowledge or knowledge from its agents, then you may be able to recover costs, even if you failed to tell the owner in writing what the owner already knew or should have known.

However, to "win" with this approach, a contractor must demonstrate that failure of written notice did the owner no harm, because the most effective course of action was taken, and the owner could not have further reduced the cost by an alternative method.

Lack of Prejudice

A contractor's failure to give written timely notice is not a viable defense for the owner when the change order request is based upon defective and deficient contract documents. The owner is responsible under the idea of implied warranty to furnish correct and accurate contract documents and is not relieved of its responsibility by lack of written notice where the cause of the problem is clearly within the control of the owner and not the fault of a contractor.

Chapter 4

Early Warnings

No single indicator or a combination of indicators (money, time, and construction methodology) can guarantee getting approval of a change order. They are only indications that a change order may be needed.

To prepare a change order, a detailed examination of the history of the project is often necessary to determine the issues involved. However, regardless of the type or cause of the issues, it's better to avoid controversy by early identification of the potential problem.

Losing Money

Loss of revenue during a project may be due to a bid that was too low, mismanagement of the project (by either the owner or the contractor), or a change order that was late or incomplete. There are various methods to price changes. However, no method, no matter how sophisticated in terms of accounting principles, will substitute for a complete and thorough system of record keeping on the job. Contractors have the burden of proving each and every element of requested extra costs. In addition to establishing the cause, there must be no other factors that may have contributed to the owner-caused problem.

To prove the losses in productivity were the responsibility of the owner, the contractor must show that the loss flowed from the owner's actions, or that reasonable folks in the position of the contractor would have foreseen the extra costs as a probable result from something the owner did or did not do.

Time

The second identifying factor of a possible construction change to the original plan is time. Reduced learning curves, generalized nonproductivity and delays are all vital signs that may indicate losses of time. However, documentation is the key to illustrating the problem that caused time delays.

During construction, few problems have a more significant financial impact than delays. Delays result in increased costs for the work directly affected and also have a disruptive effect upon overall scheduling and coordination.

At the heart of proving the actual impact of delays is the project schedule. Some contracts may include a "No Damages for Delay" clause. To suggest that only the contractor and subcontractors bear the burden and costs when something delays construction is unfair.

In addition to an analysis of the Critical Path Method (CPM) of scheduling or other type of schedule, to identify the impact of delays, for example:

- Was the learning curve detrimentally affected by the delay?
- Was productivity and efficiency affected by the delay?
- Were the trades impeded from their planned sequence of work?

Delays can be caused by either the actions or inactions of the owner, vendors or circumstances beyond anyone's control (ie. abnormal weather, strikes, acts of God, etc.). As such, delays are classified into general categories:

- Excusable – compensable (payment is due)
- Excusable – non compensable (the delay was excusable, but the owner does not owe compensation)
- Non-excusable (the contractor may be responsible for its own delay costs)

Construction Methodology

The third indicator of a potential change is the construction method, or how the contractor decided to proceed with the work. Prebid research and site investigations should include examinations for defective specifications and drawings, where dimensions don't add up or are otherwise inaccurate. Early identification of these factors and timely notification before they impact the project is invaluable.

While differences of opinion are a fact of life, patent (obvious) and/or latent (hidden) ambiguity in contract language is very problematic. Effectively, these occurrences are one of the rare instances where an owner is treated as "guilty" until proven innocent. However, there is still the responsibility to notify the owner that they are "guilty" by the process of requesting clarification of ambiguous language and/or design specifications.

The rules of construction for contract language are clear. Ambiguous language will be construed against the party who drafted or prepared it, which in most cases is the owner. However, the caveat to that rule is: an obvious ambiguity must be brought to the attention of the drafter.

Likewise, prebid verification or investigation of the site, as well as contract language, must occur with reasonable diligence. Crying wolf at a much later point in time will not convince anyone of a potential change an experienced contractor would have found by actual examination of the site.

However, the plans and specifications are warranted to be useable as offered by the owner, and it is not the duty of the contractor to verify the dimensions or location of the work.

> "...that the Contractor is a businessman usually pressed for time and should, therefore, not be required to ferret out discrepancies not readily observable from an examination of the contract bid documents." Bromley Construction Company, 72-1 BCA 9252 (1972).

Chapter 5

Changes Happen

Handling contentious issues and trouble are, often, resolved at the project level without having to go to arbitration or worse—litigation. The changes clause allows project teams to be fair, reasonable and professional.

The following are potential changes eligible for compensation and time extensions:

- Directed changes
- Constructive change
- Cardinal change
- Acceleration
- Differing site conditions
- Defective and deficient contract documents
- Weather
- Suspension
- Termination
- Delays
- Implied warranty delays
- Impossibility of performance
- Economic impossibility of performance
- Strikes
- Owner-furnished items
- Superior knowledge

Directed Changes

A directed change is the prerogative of the owner, and almost no area of the contract is unassailable. Changes can be made to the contract documents themselves, specifications, drawings or entire sections. Changes may be directed orally or in writing and as stated earlier, documentation of such directions are of paramount importance. Even what appears on the surface to be a minor change must be documented in writing by contractors as soon as possible to avoid possible trouble later in the project. Such verification serves as proof so that later requests for a change order or equitable adjustment can be supported.

Another type of directed change is a unit price contract change, which are simply made with modifications to individual line items with appropriate adjustment based on changed conditions. Lump sum contract changes are negotiated separately, with the exception of "no-cost" changes.

If a contractor and the owner are unable to agree on a price, a unilateral change order may be issued by the owner. This change order can direct contractors to continue on a unit, time and equipment, and material or force account basis. Contractors typically use RFIs to request change orders.

Time-critical changes may be directed by the owner and negotiation of the price adjustment will be completed later. Unilateral "two-part" change orders provide for interim payment and leave the remaining payment open for later negotiation. The ConsensusDocs 200 contracts allow for two-part payments.

ARTICLE 12 DISPUTE MITIGATION AND
RESOLUTION
12.1 WORK CONTINUANCE AND PAYMENT:

Constructor shall continue to the Work and maintain the schedule of the Work during any dispute mitigation or resolution procedure. If Constructor continues to perform, owner shall continue to make payments in accordance with this agreement.

The existence of a directed change is not an issue; the trouble comes from convincing the owner of the amount of payment and an extension of the time. When the owner issues a directed change, potential problems can develop in two forms:

- The owner agrees payment is necessary but doesn't agree with the amount.
- The owner asserts that the change falls within the no-cost category.

The burden of proof for the costs and impacts of changes lies with the contractor. Accounting data must be accurate, concise and readily auditable. Data should be presented positively and persuasively. As suggested, documentation through contract documents, correspondence, field notes, video, etc., can be invaluable tools in preparing the successful directed change order pricing.

Contracts may contain change order formulas; therefore, a thorough review must be made of the contract documents for analysis of pre-approved additional impact costs.

The key to receiving payment for a directed change is the characterization of the work as an extra. Make sure the requested change order is not included or detailed in the original scope of the work. In addition, a reservation of the right to claim impact or "ripple effect" damages should be noted.

Other possible concepts for a directed change are:

- Waiver, i.e., where the owner knew that the contractor considered the work to be extra but insisted upon its immediate performance or indicated that it would be covered by a future modification or change order, thereby inducing the contractor to assume the risk and perform.
- Prior course of conduct between the parties, whereby extras were paid for without a written change order.

Recovery may be allowed if the owner accepted the extra work via inspections or other acts evidencing acceptance (if they used it).

Action or inaction (either verbal or written) initiated and demanded by the owner's representative which increases the cost of the work is considered a constructive change if the contractor is required to do the work without an agreement. Any change in the schedule can have a potential cost impact.

If the schedule is lengthened, invariably costs increase. Similarly, if the schedule is shortened, there is also the potential for a cost increase (see Acceleration). However, contractors must convince the owner that the change in the work was not covered by the initial contract. Also that the change was not caused by the contractor's own inefficiency and that notification of the change was provided to the owner's representative.

Identifying the change is the contractor's challenge, and again, documentation throughout the life of the contract is the key.

Constructive Changes

Constructive describes a situation where an issue was forced by a disagreement and a demand, where the contractor is placed in a position to have to perform work that they disagree with. Constructive changes can involve interpretation of drawings and specifications.

Extra work performed at the request (demand) of the owner or owner's representative should be followed by a written document. Constructive change assertions that are not backed by a written change order must provide proof of:

- Merit and entitlement
- Cause
- Amount of time and money the change will cost

If a contractor can document the above areas, they may be able to get additional money for cost, profit and schedule impacts.

Constructive change arguments should be asserted as promptly as possible after the change in work has been identified, but before the final payment.

The owner may assert these reasons for not paying for the changes:

- Falls under minimum performance under the contract
- Work performed exceeds the established minimum
- Performance of the work was required by the owner or his agent

The better way to deal with work beyond the scope of the contract is to do the work under protest and reserve the right to payment and a time extension. Otherwise, a refusal to perform the constructive work may be found as a default, and the contract may be terminated.

While there are specific responsibilities to perform under the contract, the owner also has specific duties and obligations. These are implied warranties, and there are several types:

Implied Warranty of the Adequacy of Specifications

According to the Spearin Doctrine, the owner is responsible for the consequences of defects in the plans and specifications. Contractors are faced with at least two dilemmas when confronted with defective plans and specifications:

- Physical impossibility of performance: specifications impose unattainable requirements in a physical sense. What is being asked cannot be done by any contractor.
- Financial impracticality of performance: specifications are commercially impractical when excessive costs are required to perform satisfactory construction.

Under this implied warranty, contractors have the right to assume that owner-provided specifications are accurate and correct. The owner, in turn, accepts responsibility for accuracy of the specifications, drawings and other contract documents.

Implied Warranty to Act with Reasonable Diligence

Changes to the contract can be time-consuming, and the owner retains the responsibility to act with "reasonable diligence" in executing such changes. Failure on the part of the owner to approve a change in a timely manner can hinder forward momentum and result in the contractor getting additional time and, hopefully, money as a result of the delay.

Implied Warranty Not to Hinder the Performance of the Other Party

Related to the implied warranty to act with reasonable diligence, this warranty ensures approvals and changes of technical direction, inspection, production, etc., in a timely manner. Deliberate hindrance without just cause by the owner is grounds to ask for additional compensation.

Implied Warranty: Fitness for a Particular Purpose, Uniform Commercial Code

The Uniform Commercial Code (UCC) applies to both prime contracts and subcontracts. The owner accepts responsibility for the suitability of any items, material or goods that are individually specified to be fit for such purpose. This is particularly true with owner-furnished, contractor-installed (OFCI) material or equipment.

Contract documents aren't perfect and can have a variety of deficiencies and discrepancies, but the owner has responsibility for the documents and to assure that they are reasonably free of error. The term "reasonable" is subjective at best. Rational and careful consideration should be given to defining the deficiencies prior to a decision to file a change order. If contractors have given proper attention to detail during the pre-bid phase, identification of defects and deficiencies will be easier.

Cardinal Change

A cardinal change is an alteration of the contract where the scope of the contract was revised to an extent that the work does not look even close to the original contract. If contracted to build a basketball court, then the owner insists on a complete gymnasium, that's a cardinal change.

The key word is scope. Hopefully the scope was adequately defined (fair and reasonable) when the contract was entered into. The test is whether the work is essentially the same work as the parties bargained for when the contract was awarded.

There aren't consistent guidelines to determine whether a cardinal change has occurred. For example, the total number of changes, the frequency of the changes, the nature of the changes, and the time for the changes to be performed could indicate a cardinal change.

Each circumstance is determined by the individual facts involved, leaving contractors in a somewhat untenable position in trying to determine what will be regarded as a cardinal change. Therefore, it's best to address changes in the scope of the work under either the directed changes or constructive changes clause.

Acceleration

It's implied in contracts that the owner has the responsibility to keep a project in a state of forwardness. Once the schedule has been approved, it may or may not be followed. If the owner orders, in writing, an earlier completion for an activity or a milestone date, acceleration (speeding up of the work) is being demanded.

Similarly, where the owner does not directly order earlier completion but references termination for default and or threatens to impose liquidated damages, then you have been placed in a constructive acceleration mode due to the owner's actions.

When addressing acceleration, project teams can argue about who owns the time between when critical activities can start without delaying activities that follow it or the overall completion date (scheduled float). Float is the extra time built into a schedule that may offset unforeseen events, e.g., inclement weather. There may not be a clear answer as to who owns this time, but in general, the float time can be treated as belonging to the project itself, as opposed to the exclusive use or benefit of either party.

Contributing to the debate about ownership of float is the conflict between two common provisions in construction contracts.

First, the idea that the risk of construction lies with the contractor tends to support the owner's claim to float. This idea generally states that the unknowns of construction that cause risk are the contractor's responsibility. However, delays that reduce float cannot always be anticipated and, therefore, are part of the unknown of construction. So the argument goes that delays reducing float are the contractor's risk.

Second, the contractor is responsible for the means, methods, sequence and techniques of construction. This tends to support the contractor's claim to float. The logic is that if the contractor is responsible for the means, methods, sequence and techniques of construction, should they not also be permitted to change them by reducing or extending the time necessary to accomplish any particular activity which may result in a change in method or technique? This complicates computation of inefficiency and losses in productivity as well as direct costs unless contractors can track and identify specific causes for delays and segregate the cost incurred.

Significant cost increases may be experienced as a result of accelerated efforts. When acceleration is justified and required by the owner, an agreement should be made frequently (even weekly) regarding adequate reimbursement for those extra costs prior to commencing the work. Periodic schedule updates and progress reports will assist in verifying the costs of acceleration.

The proper tracking during each time period should include:

- Current status: where construction progress is relative to any intermediate milestones and final completion compared to the original schedule
- How current status was achieved
- How to maintain (or remedy) the current status

Some of the costs associated with acceleration may include overtime, inefficiencies, expediting costs, additional supervision, wage escalations, field overheads, fixed costs, equipment, etc.

Each instance of acceleration is considered separately, and a realistic assessment of the impact is essential. It's the contractor's responsibility to monitor and report progress. Acceleration costs must be clearly identified for them to be considered by an owner for payment. Inaccurate or speculative pricing may jeopardize work relationships and the recovery of any extra and additional costs.

The inefficiencies caused by acceleration can greatly impact the cost of construction. Such inefficiencies include significant rise and fall in labor force and productivity due to retraining, over-manning because of schedule disruptions, excessive overtime and equipment shortages or delays.

Acceleration can be either directed or constructive:

- Directed acceleration may be a written or verbal order. Doing anything based on verbal orders should be avoided and is risky.
- Constructive acceleration results from the lack of a specific response which forces the contractor to make a decision to proceed or delay construction. It is usually generated from a written request for clarification that is not answered in a timely manner. It can also be the failure to award a time extension when an added demand is made by the owner.

Differing Site Conditions or Changed Conditions

When unanticipated, differing conditions are encountered on the site that should have been outlined in the specifications and drawings, the owner is obligated to pay the additional costs associated to the adjustment.

This clause has various forms and was designed to protect contractors from unknown conditions, thereby encouraging bids which do not account for large contingencies. This clause is designed to provide a fair and equitable solution for conditions that were otherwise unknown to all parties, thus, everyone benefits from this clause. However, project teams must pay close attention to the notification requirements of the clause, which allows the owner to appraise the differing site conditions and make changes as necessary.

As stated earlier, it's the responsibility of the contractor to investigate the site prior to bidding. Change orders must be for those cases that could not have been recognized during a reasonable pre-bid investigation.

Also called changed conditions, a differing site condition usually is not visible during the site visit or pre-bid inspection. Thus, differing conditions are those sites materially dissimilar or latent (present, but not evident).

Prior to submitting a bid and to avoid utilizing the differing site changes clause in the contract, contractors should:

- Pre-bid site inspection
- Contract documents, specifications and drawings
- Technical data and knowledge
- Previous experience

Again, documentation of existing conditions during the pre-bid inspection prior to the bid is important and, as the project progresses, may become increasingly more important. Encountering differing site conditions may create a financial catastrophe for the project. Therefore, an assessment of the risks should be performed before the bid is submitted. Is there a changed condition clause, and are there exculpatory clauses in the contract i.e., language limiting the owner's responsibility for incorrect subsurface condition information?

The extent to which a contractor can get paid because of unexpected subsurface conditions depends on the inclusion of a changed condition clause in the contract. Such a clause improves the chances a contractor will get paid for unanticipated and unforeseen subsurface conditions.

However, the likelihood of success under this clause depends upon:

- The extent to which the owner has made representations or furnished information as to the conditions
- The degree to which the conditions differed materially from those represented
- Whether a prudent contractor could have anticipated the differing conditions, e.g. by a site visit or previous experience in the same geographic area
- Whether the owner had or should have had knowledge of the conditions actually encountered
- How timely the contractor provided notice to the owner when the differing site condition was discovered

Changed conditions are often classified by different types. The Type 1 condition is defined as one in which actual conditions encountered differ materially from those represented in the contract. A Type 2 condition is defined as one in which the actual conditions encountered differ materially from conditions ordinarily encountered and generally recognized to exist; for example, an aquifer in an area not previously known to contain aquifers.

There is significant experience for the Type 1 conditions, but Type 2 conditions are less frequently found. Changed condition clauses can minimize the "gambler approach" in bidding subsurface work, so that an owner may be held liable for subsurface conditions, such as abandoned electrical conduit, pipe or concrete structures below the surface, which were known to the owner. Hardly ever is it, "You bid it. You bought it."

Defective and Deficient Documents

Defects and deficiencies in contract documents occur, and the liability for errors and/or omissions lies with the drafter, which is usually the owner's designer. Recognized industry standards for evaluating the designer's responsibility are ordinary care, skill and diligence, and the reasonable person test.

United States vs. Spearin 248 U.S, 132 (1918)

> But if the contractor is bound to build according to plans and specifications prepared by the owner, the contractor will not be responsible for the consequences of defects in the plans and specifications…This responsibility of the owner is not overcome by the usual clauses requiring builders to visit the site, to check the plans, and to inform themselves of the requirements of the work…

Accompanying the owner's responsibility for reasonably accurate contract documents is the contractor's duty to include an allowance for insignificant errors, remembering that what is reasonable and/or insignificant is subjective. An experienced contractor cannot always just rely upon owner-prepared specifications if the contractor knew or should have known that the specifications could not produce the desired result. No one has the right to consciously build a useless thing (malicious obedience) and charge the owner. Therefore, contractors are expected to include an allowance for reasonable and foreseeable changes in the plans and specifications.

As previously discussed under Differing Site Condition, contractors have a duty to inquire about an obvious ambiguity. Likewise, there's an expectation to inquire when faced with the discrepancies within the contract drawings and specifications, as opposed to conflicts between the separate drawings.

Again, defective plans and specifications constitute a waiver of the notice requirement with respect to changes in the contract documents. So, if the owner inserts an exculpatory clause (relieving them of responsibility for accuracy of the plans and specifications), it may give the owner little, if any, protection.

In general, defective specifications involve clear errors, conflicts between different areas of the specifications or drawings, or the omission of important facts. A common example of defective specifications is found when a conflict exists between the specifications and drawings or between different version of the specifications or drawings.

Drawings can be deemed defective for failing to indicate exactly what they describe. However, an owner may remedy this situation when they clearly indicate that the drawings do not show all items of the required work. Should the owner make such a demand and should that demand conflict with other areas, then look at the order of precedent provisions to seek clarification.

Weather

Change order requests based on weather must be able to demonstrate that the weather varied significantly and directly impacted the progress of the project, disregarding other factors. However, the weather must be unusually severe for the locality and the time of year involved in the contract. Contractors must also show to what extent the weather delayed the specific work. Usually, costs associated with a full seasonal shift of work due to weather are compensable, e.g., having to perform work in the winter's cold or summer's heat, if it was planned for the opposite season.

Even if the weather does not reach the statistical level of severity in the region, a contractor can win if they can prove the impact of the weather on the work was unusually severe or highly unusual. For example, if a roofing contractor was required to install a roof using a method of dry application, and the weather, while not severe, presented moisture that prevented progress, the contractor is probably entitled to extra money or time extension.

Suspension

Usually, only the owner can declare a suspension of work, or work stoppage. To be called suspension, the duration must be long enough to significantly impact the project.

In federal government contracts, compensation is limited to actual costs for labor, material and equipment expenses. Generally, no profit is allowed on suspension claims. During the suspension period, contractors are responsible for reducing costs to the absolute minimum possible.

With nonfederal contracts, generally compensation is calculated by establishing value and profit, within reasonable guidelines. The owner can suspend work, but criteria for compensation should be firmly established by a specific format for costs via the suspensions clause in the contract.

Constructive suspension occurs when:

- Delays in providing information about utilities that forced a contractor to perform the work in a different manner
- Unreasonable delays in responding to requests for information or clarification
- Issuing changes necessitated by defective plans and specifications

In effect, contractors are placed in a "no go" situation because of the owner's inaction which prohibits a contractor from continuing work effectively. It can be argued that a constructive suspension of work is a constructive change.

Whatever the situation, the result should provide contractors with compensation for standby labor, materials, equipment and overhead.

Termination

Contract provisions that allow the owner to terminate a contractor most frequently, but not exclusively, occur in federal government contracts. Contractors can be terminated for failing to complete the work on time, refusing to complete the project with adequate diligence or if it is not considered in the best interest of the owner to complete the contract (referred to as a termination for convenience).

Termination for Default

The most undesirable form of termination is termination for default. In this case, a contractor's reputation is placed in jeopardy and future projects and bonding capacity may be lost as a result. Termination for default should be avoided at all costs, and an alternative solution should always be actively pursued.

The threat to terminate the contract for default, where the owner's representative knew of an excusable delay, most likely constitutes a constructive acceleration order. It's analogous to coercion.

Two basic defenses to a termination for default are:

- Substantial performance
- Owner's abuse of discretion

Substantial performance, while not full and complete performance, is very close to what was bargained for by the parties, and contractors are entitled to the contract price, as adjusted for the uncompleted work. This concept is intended to protect contractors who have proceeded in good faith and honestly endeavored to complete the terms of the contract.

The owner is granted broad administrative discretion to make the decision to terminate for default. Normally, there is no second-guessing of an administrative decision to terminate for default, provided that the facts justifying the termination do not constitute an abuse of discretion. To establish an abuse of discretion requires extensive documentation. Collect fact-preservation memos from everyone involved including subcontractors, suppliers and others regarding such improper or unreasonable actions.

Upon termination, the owner must send a written notice to the contractor specifying type, effective date and the extent of the termination. In turn, contractors are required to notify the subcontractors and suppliers in the same manner.

Accounting records are utilized to determine actual costs and profit due and owed. This type of termination can be complicated and time-consuming, involving extensive audits, administrative effort and contract research. Upper management, an attorney and consulting experts should be brought on board when preparing the position and change order request that supports the negating of the owner's termination notice.

There are two approaches to cost recovery after termination: inventory and total cost. The total cost approach maximizes cost recovery, in contrast to the inventory method, which limits costs to work in place and purchased materials.

Termination for Convenience

The termination for convenience concept was developed as a means to wind down the massive procurement efforts that accompanied major world wars. However, over time, this concept has been extended to construction and supply contracts. In no other area has such a complete escape been provided for parties to a contract. In essence, this all-encompassing clause grants the owner the right to terminate any contract without cause.

Further, the right to recovery is limited to actual costs incurred, profit on work done, and costs preparing the termination settlement proposal. Anticipated profit recovery is prohibited. Such cost recovery limitations are generally contained in a standard termination for convenience clause. Generally such clauses are not found in commercial contracts with the exception of the ConsensusDocs.

Although the owner's right to terminate is broadly construed, the owner's representative must exercise discretion when considering terminating for convenience. The exercise of discretion in termination for convenience is discouraged where such a decision would demonstrate bad faith, an elusive term and difficult to demonstrate. In certain cases, a termination for default may be converted to a termination for convenience, if there are valid reasons or defenses for nonperformance.

Delays

Contract terms and conditions generally specify that a project be completed with a certain number of calendar delays. A project that is not fully complete by this deadline normally will experience trouble because somebody is losing money. It makes sense that whoever caused the delay should be responsible for paying for it. The issue is proving who was responsible for the delay and how the delay impacted the project. Unless a party to the contract wants to confess, sorting out "who done it" requires examining each activity and a careful analysis of the schedule(s).

As discussed earlier, delays can be simplified somewhat by categorizing them into three general areas:

- Excusable
- Non-Excusable
- Compensable

Excusable Delays

When a contractor is in no way at fault and has absolutely no control over the delay, the delay is considered excusable. Some examples may include acts of God like weather, floods, storms; owner-furnished item delays; labor disputes; or a strike.

Extensions of time are the sole remedy for delays beyond a contractor's control.

Non-Excusable Delays

When the contractor and subcontractors or suppliers are at fault or negligent because of lack of project coordination or failure to have equipment and material delivered in a timely manner (except owner-furnished items), the delay is considered non-excusable. Non-excusable delays may allow the owner to recover costs associated with loss of income, additional finance costs, additional architect, engineering and management costs, and lost income potential. A contractor may also be responsible for liquidated damages and compensation regarding loss of business or owner's charges.

Compensable Delays

Compensable delays are those caused by or arising from actions or inactions of the owner, and the contractor is unable to control the circumstances surrounding the delay. Some examples include failure of the owner to approve shop drawings in a timely manner, design changes and holds, and limited site access.

Contractors can recover standby costs in addition to the direct and indirect costs associated with such delays. Examples of compensable damages include increased overhead, wages, escalation or inefficiency. Such delays should result in a time extension as well as additional money.

The contract documents generally allow a way to determine compensable delays. Not all time extensions will automatically result in an allowable reimbursement, but the American Institute of Architects (AIA) general conditions allow a contractor to recover some delay costs.

U.S. Government Standard Contract Form 23A provides a means for the contractor to recover in an "Equitable Adjustment" for some delay costs. Equitable adjustment is the federal government's term for change order. Types of delays may include reimbursement for additional equipment costs, material escalation, extended overhead and profit, additional finance costs and field overhead.

Regardless of the method used to recover the additional costs resulting from the delay, contractors must prove exactly how the job progressed, including planned and as-built schedules.

The concept of delay is a companion to acceleration and suspension of work. Contractors may have delays coupled with acceleration as well as delays associated with a work suspension. These concepts are not mutually exclusive and should be considered in terms of which party is at fault for the action causing the delay.

Concurrent Delays

When two or more delays occur caused by both the owner and contractor at the same point in time, these are called concurrent delays. In the case of a concurrent delay, the remedy is to allow a time extension with contractors bearing their own losses. However, that depends on which party started the delay (primacy), how long it lasted and how long they ran parallel, i.e. occurring at the same time.

Frequently, a contract will contain a "no damage for delay clause," which entitles a contractor to receive time extensions only and no money for delay damages. Contractors may avoid the impact of that clause by showing:

- Active interference by the owner
- Bad faith or arbitrary action by the owner
- Lack of site availability or right-of-way availability
- Reasonability unforeseeable delay

Impossibility or Impracticability of Performance

Impossibility or impracticability of performance is when the situation is challenged by extreme and unreasonable difficulty, expense, injury or loss. This is not to say that performance will (or will not) be excused when greater difficulty or expense that was originally anticipated by either party is encountered. Instead, this allows both parties protection from absolute unknowns and essentially allows for total revision of the contract if these conditions exist.

It's difficult to demonstrate practical impossibility. The particular facts and circumstances must be analyzed to determine whether the owner required something that later proves impossible or whether the contractor has assumed the risk of impossibility. Since this is usually so difficult to document, the better course of action may be to consider presenting an alternative form of change (e.g., constructive).

This concept has been discussed previously as a violation of the idea of implied warranties. To prove impossibility, contractors must establish that there was no way any other contractor could have performed the work requested or that the work was physically impossible to perform in a way that met the desired specifications.

Economic Impossibility of Performance

Economic impossibility of performance is a subclass of subjective impossibility of performance. It's a related hardship, where there is unreasonable difficulty or expense. In this case, performance can be excused. The impossibility of performance usually must be in the thing to be done (objective impossibility) and not in the inability of the contractor (subjective impossibility) to do it.

The Uniform Commercial Code (UCC 2-615) has three conditions:
1. A contingency has occurred
2. The contingency has made performance impractical
3. The nonoccurrence of that contingency was a basic assumption in the contract

Other considerations:

- There can be no other cause
- The trouble must be beyond the control of the parties and not be predictable and unavoidable
- Notice must be provided to the owner
- The economic basis is so radically different that the contract would clearly exceed what the parties could reasonably expect

Strikes

Strikes are usually an excusable delay. Unsanctioned or "wildcat" strikes are not. The same rules pertain to a strike against a subcontractor or supplier that affects the prime contractor. The rule also applies where a jurisdictional strike against an unrelated contractor prevents the workforce from reaching their jobs because of a picket line. However, the rule does not recognize a contractor's inability to find or keep skilled personnel as an excuse.

If the owner precipitated the strike, a contractor will probably get paid and receive a time extension.

To demonstrate an excusable delay for a strike, a contractor must show that they acted reasonably by not precipitating or prolonging the strike and took steps to avoid its effects.

Except for a strike, contractors are probably not going to be excused for labor difficulties, loss of key personnel or an unexpected labor shortage. Contractors have assumed the risk of hiring and maintaining a qualified workforce.

An exception might be where contractors experience a shortage due to hiring acts (higher salaries) of a competitor; however, this is a very unusual circumstance.

Owner-furnished Items

Defects and/or delayed delivery of owner-furnished and contractor-installed equipment or materials (OFCI) can provide the basis for time extension and payment. Timing is key; what could a contractor reasonably anticipate? This type of trouble can become a full-scale exercise in contract interpretation.

Delay by the owner in furnishing materials or equipment generally gives rise to an extension of time under the default-delay clause but may or may not permit a contractor to get paid because of the delay, depending upon the terms of the contract and whether the terms constitute an expressed or implied warranty on the part of the owner. This concept has been previously discussed under the implied warranty to cooperate and not hinder a contractor.

Where the owner commits to furnishing certain items, the owner is deemed to have assumed the risk for delivery of property or materials. Where no specific date is stated in the contract, the owner should supply it in time to maintain the schedule. The burden of proving an excusable reason for delayed delivery is on the owner. The owner should act reasonably when supplying OFCI. A contractor may be able to get both a time extension for late delivery as well as money for losses experienced as a result of the delay.

Superior Knowledge

When the owner possesses necessary information that would avoid trouble and doesn't say anything, the owner violates an implied warranty. The contract specifications can also be deemed defective when the owner does not disclose in the specifications or other bidding documents any particular, significant difficulties or technical problems of which the owner has knowledge.

The following key elements must be established in order for the superior knowledge to apply:

- The owner knew, or should have known, the vital information and its probable consequences at the time the contract was awarded
- The contractor or subcontractors neither knew, nor should have known, the vital information and its probable consequences at the time the contract was awarded
- The owner was either aware of, or should have been aware of, the contractor's lack of knowledge but nevertheless failed to disclose the pertinent information
- The owner intentionally failed to disclose the pertinent information to mislead everyone

Summary

Managing construction contracts requires contractors to:

- Read and understand the terms and conditions of the contract
- Do what it requires when it's supposed to get done
- Promptly identify anything that is different than what is supposed to be built or constructed
- Notify the owner using the method defined in the contract (read as: "in writing")

- Document facts, keep track of costs and time, and present changes to the owner is a sensible, reasonable way

Chapter 6

Calculating the Cost of Changes

A problem for owners, designers and particularly contactors is how to reasonably calculate the costs involved when the project runs into trouble—when changes are being made. Figuring out who is responsible and how to settle up almost always is a problem. Calculating construction inefficiencies and losses in productivity can be complicated and often based solely on opinions or even a wild imagination.

The following methods for calculating inefficiencies and losses in construction productivity have been used by contractors, owners, design professionals and attorneys in a variety of ways:

- Satisfying a curiosity about construction costs under changing circumstances
- Gathering general information
- Assisting negotiations
- Preparing change orders
- Resolving contract disputes
- Allowing project stakeholders the opportunity to understand the cost implications of their decisions before committing to a direction

All the methods used here were derived from recognized and often used data and information. More detailed research is ongoing but familiar information that's been accepted in the construction industry was purposely used.

The examples for calculating the cost of changes are for specific conditions. The best way to be anywhere close to accurate is to compare what was planned to what actually happened. The difficulty is gathering the planned versus actual data, determining the cause and effect, and assigning liability. Knowing the basis, baseline, standard and accurate as-planned data is a good starting point. The key to calculating the difference is to know what was planned and what actually happened and then calculating the costs.

One of the earliest tools for calculating the effects of construction changes is the Corps of Engineers 415, the U.S. Army Corps of Engineers, the Modification Impact Evaluation Guide EP-415-1-3-1 July 1979. However, it has fallen from favor by some contractors and government contracting officers. The reason for disfavor may be any of these:

- It was becoming too expensive for the government to include all the costs in change orders using the methods in the guide
- The original research used to develop the guide was not very sound
- Some combination of the above

Other industry standards are often cited in change orders and in federal government contracting. Requests for Equitable Adjustments (REAs) are used to estimate the effect that changes can have on the overall project, including the work that is not part of the change order.

Construction contracts may be different with respect to the recovery of inefficiency costs as previously discussed, but many, if not all, require specific notice requirements and a method for the allocation and justification of additional costs. Solely using construction industry "standards" after-the-fact to justify a request for what some call "impact costs" can get everyone into more trouble. It's difficult to reconstruct the events of a project and associate them with additional costs after-the-fact. A contractor's best bet is to use these industry standards to justify the reasonableness of the costs of the changes before they occur.

Again, inefficiency and loss of productivity damages are often included in change orders on construction projects. An assertion for loss of productivity or inefficiency is a claim by a contractor that its costs increased due to actions or inactions of the owner.

Contractors have the burden of proving the need for a change order as well as the validity of the amount. Again, as soon as possible after a delay or disruption occurs (which may give rise to inefficiency or loss of productivity costs), contractors should provide notice to the owner and establish detailed records to segregate the additional costs involved.

The responsible and genuine way to discuss recovering losses in productivity is by directly connecting the actions of the owner (the cause) to the resultant extra costs incurred (the effect) and link the two together with certainty. Cost records correlated to each owner-caused disruption or delay leading to losses in productivity and inefficiency of operations are the best way to demonstrate extra costs. Accurate cost records also increase the chances of surviving an audit of extra and additional costs.

When an owner-caused event affects the planned means, method or sequence of construction, identify the problem and give written notification to the owner immediately if there are additional costs. Advise the owner that the additional costs will be invoiced, but that they will be kept to a minimum. In addition to the cost accounting changes, impress upon the project team the need to produce accurate, complete and timely daily reports to document:

- Job conditions
- Where work occurred
- Quantities installed; how much work is being done
- The resources used (labor, equipment, materials, subcontractors)
- Owner-caused problems

Again, contractors should create new cost codes (labor, equipment, materials and subcontracts) to capture direct costs and introduce new activities into the CPM network schedule or extend durations for those activities that were affected. This will help capture the indirect costs that invariably occur. Preparing a variance analysis using solid data will make it easier to present by not having to rely on speculative costs. In short, contractors won't have to guess or, worse yet, manufacture costs.

In the field, especially on fast-moving projects, these procedures do not always happen, as it's sometimes difficult to recognize the symptoms when they occur. Because of this, various methods and approaches have been used to prove damages.

As mentioned previously, several industry standards are frequently referenced or cited to prove the existence of damages and extra costs (e.g. Department of the Army's Modification Impact Evaluation Guide EP-415-1-3-2 July 1979.) These standards were to be used primarily for estimating the impact costs on unchanged work before the authorization of a change.

The Mechanical Contractor Association of America (MCAA) series of management methods bulletins, particularly Bulletin 58 (1976), discusses factors affecting productivity. The bulletin includes a list of factors that negatively affect projects but cautions that the sixteen factors are intended to serve only as a reference and should be tested by work experience. The factors are necessarily arbitrary and can vary from project to project.

The Business Roundtable, BR (1980), "Schedules Overtime Effect on Construction Projects" illustrates the losses of productivity that can occur when overtime is scheduled. The study demonstrates that, after reaching a certain threshold, losses in productivity occurs, and overtime is no longer cost efficient and effective.

A common mistake when using any one of the many studies to validate or justify cost overrun damages is to compare a project to a standard and simply say that damages are proven. At the very least, the circumstances and conditions of the cited study and the "damaged" project should be similar.

The combination of effective notice to the owner, schedule revisions, accurate daily reports and auditable job costs records will generally ensure that, all things being equal, the request for a change order receives a favorable review. Because impact costs do not always manifest themselves immediately, having reliable records and using industry studies to support a request for damages will make a presentation more credible, enhancing chances of getting paid. Understanding the limits of using construction industry standards is important.

Directed Changes

There are two ever-present axioms in construction:

- There will be directed changes on engineering and building construction projects.
- There will be different opinions about the effect of the directed changes on the cost and schedule of the project.

A directed change is any event initiated by an owner that results in a modification of the project work and or affects the planned schedule. When changes are introduced into an ongoing project, the effects on a project's productivity depend on the amount of changes (how many) and the timing of their introduction.

- Productivity drops rapidly as the frequency of interruptions increases.
- Almost any discontinuity in the normal flow of work negatively affects productivity.
- Productivity is directly and inversely proportional to the cost of the change.

> *When changes are introduced into an ongoing project, the effects on a project's productivity depend on the amount of changes (how many) and the timing of their introduction.*

A directed change can be an increase or decrease in the type or scope of work or work for which there is no original scope. A directed change can also be a delay, compression or acceleration of existing work with no new work added or deleted.

These factors may contribute to the impact that changes have on projects:

- How many additional working man-hours will be required?
- How much administrative time (away from the work) will be necessary for the ordering and delivery of any new material and/or equipment?
- How much additional time will be required to incorporate the change?

- How much schedule float or slack time is consumed by the change?
- What impact will the change have on the current critical path (a more tightly scheduled project may be more affected by changes than one with larger amounts of initial float)?
- When will the change be introduced into the workflow?
- Will additional equipment be needed to implement the change?
- Should additional equipment be rented or purchased?
- What resources (i.e., equipment, tools) will be diverted from other work to implement the change?
- How much additional manpower will be required?
- How much of a learning curve will be experienced?
- What work-in-progress will have to change to accommodate the proposed changed work?
- Will existing or recently installed work have to be demolished or reworked to accommodate the changed work?
- Will ongoing or planned work have to be accelerated, slowed, re-sequenced or suspended in order to economically install the new work?
- Will trades be stacked on each other?
- Will there be congestion caused by trade stacking?

There are a variety of factors that can determine when (or if) the introduction of a change will have an irrevocable, unrecoverable, long-term effect on the finances of a project. Again, the timing and frequency of proposed change orders have a great deal to do with the outcome of the changed work and the project as a whole.

The Construction Industry Institute (CII) measured the effect that the frequency of changes had on various construction projects. This study utilized Productivity Index (PI) to track workers hours along with the number of changes. Not surprisingly, the CII study concluded (as was already known intuitively by most contractors) that there is a direct correlation between losses in productivity and the frequency of disturbances. As a result, an extreme number of disturbances introduced at one time can reduce productivity to less than half of standard performance.

Another study to isolate and quantify the effects of changes titled, "The Effects of Change Orders on Productivity," examined 90 specific cases or instances where losses in productivity were experienced on 57 projects. The goal of the study was to determine reasons for and the sources of factors that affect losses of productivity. The study researched the individual cases and the projects and determined that there was a linear relationship between the percentage of change orders and the loss of productivity. It concluded that change orders have a detrimental and cumulative effect on labor productivity when the total labor hours spent on change orders exceeded 10-15 percent of the labor hours for the original contract.

This particular finding is of interest because it allows a threshold to be determined for the impact of changes. As a result of this research, if changes approach 10-15 percent of the labor value of the contract, then significant global losses in productivity will, in all likelihood, become evident, and there is a high potential for extra costs.

The following chart (Figure 6.1), which has been modified for clarity, can serve as an early warning system to facilitate the project team's "early detection, early cure" of problems. It can alert project teams to the potential impacts related to changes and allow modification of project procedures to account for the cumulative effect.

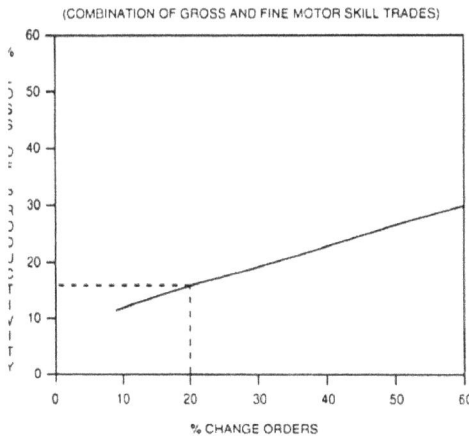

6.1. Modified from the original found in "The Effects of Change Orders on Productivity" by Charles A. Leonard

The horizontal axis indicates the percent of the total contract hours added as change orders.

- The vertical axis is the resulting loss of productivity.
- The intersection of X and Y is approximately 16%.

Applying the 16 percent inefficiency rating documented by Charles A. Leonard, change costs can be estimated in advance to influence whether the change is worth undertaking.

Example 6.1

Twenty-five electricians are scheduled to work forty hours a week for a total of 1,000 hours.

In a two-week period, the owner introduces a variety of changes expected to increase the planned hours for that period by 20 percent (an additional 400 hours).

Let's assume the hourly cost is $35 per hour.

We will also assume no premium is paid for overtime in this example.

Scheduled = (2 weeks x 40 hours/week) x 25 electricians x $35/hr= $70,000

Add 20 percent (400 hours) in change orders = 2,400 hours x $35/hr =$84,000

Account for 16 percent inefficiency = 2,400 – 16% (384 hours) = 2,016 efficient hours

Paying for 2,400 hours but only getting 2,016 worth of efficient work

Loss of $13,440 ($84,000 (2,400 paid) - $70,560 (2,016 efficient work))

Interpreting the effect of the added changes on the unchanged work and the project overall may not be as simple as the above example, but the negative effects of added changes are genuine. The studies (and experience) demonstrate that stopping and restarting work, changing up tools, stocking, staging, moving materials, relocating and reconfiguring crews all add to global losses in productivity and create inefficiencies.

Studies cannot be indiscriminately or universally applied to construction projects to prove inefficiencies and losses in productivity. Doing so would be a misuse of the research and a disservice to the efforts of the researchers. However, the research does identify that changes can, in fact, seriously affect the success of a construction project, and changes should be issued and undertaken with circumspection.

Overtime

The US Army Corps of Engineers developed the Modification Impact Evaluation Guide because of the "lack of guidance or experience in developing reasonably reliable estimates of cost/time for impact on the unchanged work before the fact."

In developing the manual, the Corps was responding to the changes in the Defense Acquisition Regulation (DAR) requiring consideration of all costs when developing change-order estimates. One of the primary impacts researched was the effects of overtime on construction project productivity (Figure 6.2).

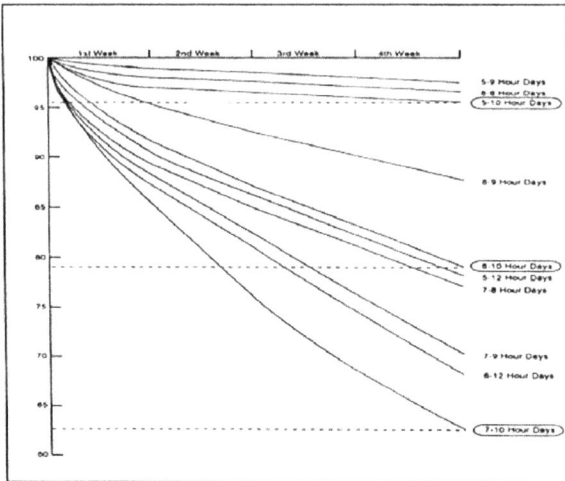

Figure 6.2. Effect of Work Schedule on Efficiency
Modification Impact Evaluation Guide, EP415-1-3

The Business Round Table also developed data to aid in measuring (predicting) the effect of overtime on productivity. Calculating the cumulative effects of overtime work on efficiency using the Business Roundtable data (Figure 6.3) can help determine the total cost of overtime in addition to the premium customarily paid for overtime.

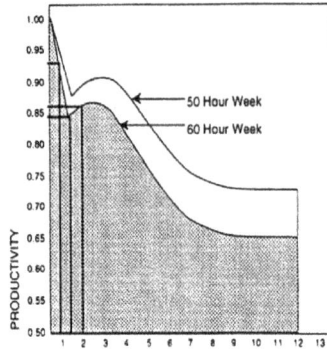

Figure 6.3. Cumulative Effect of Overtime on Productivity from "The Business Roundtable"

Using some of the same data found in Table 6-1 below, an owner issues change orders that will delay related work and requests crews work overtime to compensate for the time lost due to the change orders. During the weeks of September 20 and September 27, the owner authorizes two continuous weeks of time-and-one-half or 60-hour workweeks. Use the Business Roundtable Graph (Figure 6.3) to calculate the total impact outlined in Table 6-1.

	A.	B.	C.	D.	E. Percent	F.
Week Ending	Planned Crew Size	Planned Man-hours	Revised Man-hours	Percent Productive	Production Lost	Inefficient Hours
Sept 6, 2030						
Sept 13, 2030						
Sept 20, 2030	165	1320	1980	.93	.07	138.6
Sept 27, 2030	170	1360	1020	.86	.14	142.8
			1020	.84	.16	163.2
Oct 4, 2030						
Oct 11, 2030						
						444.6

Table 6.1. Example data

Two calculations are necessary for the second week. During that week, as adjustments are made, a sharp decline in productivity is experienced in the first half of the week. The owner should recognize and compensate the contractor for **$15,783.30** in addition to the premium of approximately $17.75 added to the last four hours of a twelve-hour day. Calculate premium hours by dividing $33.50 by 2 to get the dollar value of the premium time, then multiply that amount by the time-and-one-half hours. Time-and-one-half hours are calculated by subtracting planned man-hours from revised man-hours.

Example 6.2.[1]

Total Inefficient manhours	444.6 hours
Composite crew hourly rate	x $35.50
Total inefficient compensation	$15,783.30

Example 6.3.

Time and one-half

Sept 20: 1980 planned hours - 1320 revised hours = 660 hours
Sept 27: 2040 planned hours - 1360 revised hours = 680 hours
Premium hours = 1,340 hours

Premium time equals: $35.50/2 = $17.75 per hour
Premium cost equals: $17.75 x 1,340 hours = $23,785

In addition to the premium cost of $23,785, the sum of $15,783.30 should be included in the change order for inefficiency lost to the overtime.

Various industry studies exist regarding 50, 60, and 70-hour workweeks and their influence on productivity and efficiency. Understanding the industry studies can help estimators formulate bids or change order proposals.

---

1   The examples cited are not necessarily related to construction contracts and are used to demonstrate how change cost accounting is viewed by the government.

Contractors can also use the studies to evaluate projects that, for whatever reason, have fallen behind schedule. When a project falls behind, the possibility of getting a time extension is nonexistent and liquidated or actual damages are looming on the horizon, how should you sort out and evaluate the various correction options? Contractors have options available for estimating the loss of productivity and/ or efficiency due to extended overtime periods, which can apply to, or supplement, existing productivity data. Understanding the impact of overtime on productivity and efficiency is crucial to recovering lost time.

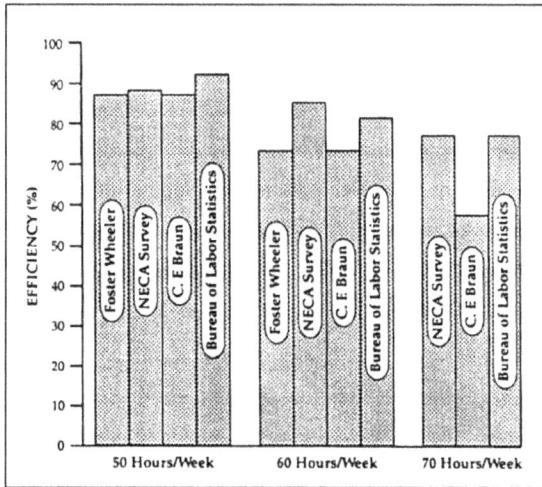

Figure 6.4. Efficiency for 50, 60, and 70-hour work weeks

Increasing manpower through the use of additional shifts rather than overtime presents unique problems. The approach is not without its limitations and drawbacks. For instance, a nightshift can mean working under artificial light, with a possible significant reduction of visibility. Working at night on the second or even a third shift may also entail working in colder weather.

Additional manpower and shift reconfigurations may require that management or field supervision overlap between the shifts to ensure continuity. There may be additional costs incurred to expedite materials, tools, and equipment to ensure that they're available when needed by those added shifts. In addition, arrangements may have to be made for the owner's representatives, inspectors, and perhaps the architect and/or engineer to be present as the work continues with "extra innings under the lights."

Choosing specific activities on, or approaching, the critical path and selectively applying resource (i.e., manpower, material, and equipment) in a metered, controlled way is the best method to "crash" a schedule and get back on track.

Again, a variety of options or combinations of options are available. Each choice has its advantages and disadvantages, including inherent losses in productivity, inefficiencies, and additional costs. Therefore, contractors can choose from any combination of the following:

- Overtime for the existing manpower
- Additional manpower on the same shift
- Additional manpower on different shifts
- Additional manpower on overtime

There are very real limits for the use of overtime. Simply put, beyond a given point, it doesn't work. The point at which the benefits are neutralized, where the cost-to-benefit ratio is low and reaches a point of diminishing return, however, is open to debate.

Researchers have examined the problem of what to do to regain project schedules and compared drawbacks associated with the various overtime shift configurations. A paper in the American Society of Civil Engineers' Journal of Construction Engineering and Management, "Effects of Schedule Overtime on Labor Productivity" reviewed available construction literature and studies previously prepared on the effects of scheduled overtime on labor productivity.

Figure 6.4 consolidates the findings for scheduled overtime for 50, 60 and 70 hours per week. The research suggests that no single study is more reliable than another. The truth, then, must be in selective use of a combination of all the studies. Again, these studies also have utility in that, together, they bracket the effect of scheduled overtime on productivity within a range and are unanimous in their general conclusions.

Table 6.2, taken from the various studies, represents the mean loss efficiency for scheduled overtime:

50-Hour Week	60-Hour Week	70-Hour Week
88%	78%	71%

Table 6.2. Efficiency for 50, 60, ad 70-hour work weeks

Any calculation or estimate for extended work periods using a 60-hour workweek should include a 22 percent loss of efficiency. Schedule activity duration calculations should also be adjusted, because time and a half is not really time and a half. Merely calculating the "absolute," non-factored duration without considering losses in productivity will cause activity duration to exceed estimates every time.

50-Hour Week	60-Hour Week	70-Hour Week
95.5%	79%	63%

Table 6.3. Efficiency for 50, 60, ad 70-hour work weeks up to four weeks

Table 6-3 demonstrates that the results are similar to the other studies, at least up to four weeks, after which the data is either not provided or does not exist.

Allowing for inaccuracies due to visually identifying points on the graph at Figure 6.4, the data is similar to other studies on acceleration. When estimating the effect of scheduled overtime, productivity rates should be adjusted accordingly. When attempting to accelerate a project that has been delayed, projected completion dates should also be adjusted to take into account the inherent losses in productivity when activities are put into 50, 60, or 70-hour workweeks. Recognizing the overall effect of overtime can make change-order estimates and completion projections more accurate and reliable.

The statistical data used by the MCAA, National Electrical Contractors Association (NECA), and the R. S. Means Company, Inc., to calculate the effect of overtime on efficiency and productivity is very similar to data published by the Business Roundtable. Each of the four cited references are accepted industry standards. What the Business Roundtable MCAA, NECA, and perhaps the Means studies really prove is that productivity increases with the reduction or elimination of overtime.

This demonstrates that overtime is only effective for short periods; three weeks seems to be the limit. When delays and disruptions occur on a project, the duration (the time it takes) for remaining work activities may be compressed, and contractors are often compelled to accelerate completion of the work. If the owner does not provide appropriate time extensions, there's the choice of not accelerating and facing the imposition of liquidated damages. The other choice is to accelerate and incur the cost of increasing resources on the project while the responsibility for the delays is resolved.

Crowding

To accelerate work, a contractor may increase crew sizes working within a limited area. If the work is **inefficient**, it's called crowding. Crowding can occur as part of an accelerated work effort, but it may complicate work as trade contractors compete for workspace and priority.

Crowding is a measure of congestion, physical conflict, and confusion between trades based upon the amount of accessible area to work in, and sometimes relates to problems with the other crafts, also referred to as trade stacking. To sample the effect of crowding, move two co-workers into an office or pickup truck and see how that affects their ability to get work completed.

Inefficiencies resulting from crowding differ from crew overloading. Crowding directly affects all craftspeople, while crew loading affects the ability to manage a single work force.

Isolating the effect and measuring the inefficiency costs of crowding is difficult and requires measuring the change from the productivity of the smaller crew to the productivity experienced by the larger crew in the same area. Two primary methods are recognized for measuring the effects of crowding: before the work is performed and after. The crowding study cited previously can be used to estimate an increase in the unit price when the job-site conditions change by adding to the workforce and available work areas are limited. Another method is to re-estimate the work based on new assumptions caused by the conditions on the project.

Because of the difficulty of precisely predicting losses in productivity associated with crowding, contractors (and subcontractors) can reserve their rights to submit change orders for additional inefficiency costs after proceeding with the work. Using the actual costs of the extra labor required is more accurate.

To measure additional labor performance on the project, there are at least two ways to come up with the crowding cost: compare actual labor usage against the construction estimate or against the resource-loaded, baseline schedule.

The construction estimate and control budget define the expected productivity or unit rates and, therefore, the cost of the work. The resource-loaded, baseline schedule should incorporate expected productivity or unit rates to establish the resources necessary to accomplish each activity. These key project records are used to allocate a portion of the actual labor variance, after-the-fact, to the actions of the owner or another team partner. This option requires calculating the unit rate cost for installation before the addition of new workers and then calculating the unit rate cost after the additional workers were added to the job. The difference in these two rates or costs could be assigned to inefficiency due to crowding.

The following is an example of a forward-priced change order proposal negotiated before any impacts due to crowding. In the construction of a 60,000 square foot structure, the original estimate and baseline schedule required 25 electricians to finish the electrical work within the original performance period.

However, the project encountered construction delays, and the electrical work had to be accelerated; therefore, 37 electricians were assigned to complete the building. The optimal number of electricians was originally 25; the number of electricians increased to 30 in the first week, increased to 34 the next week, and increased to 37 the third week (See Table 6.4).

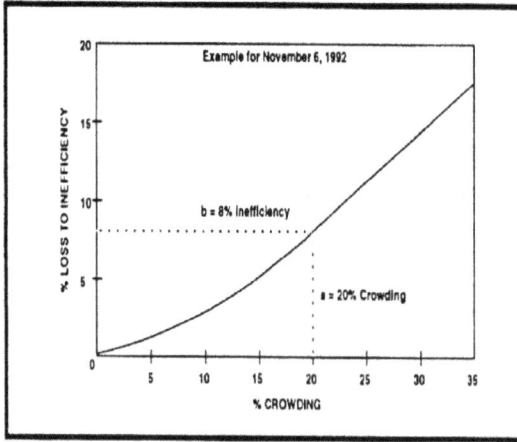

*Figure 6.5. Source: Modification Impact Evaluation
Guide, DOA EP 415-3, July 1979*

Using the Department of Army, Office of Chief Engineers Modification Impact Evaluation Guide, EP 415-1-3, July 1979, the steps for calculating lost efficiency costs due to crowding are:

- Establish the crew size which an area can efficiently accommodate (which may not necessarily be the planned crew size, however, in this example, it is 25).
- Calculate the effective/optimal crew size and new crew size for the impacted time period (Table 6.4, Columns A and B).

	A Optimal Crew Size	B New Crew Size	C Increased Crew Size	D Percent Crowding (c + a)	E Percent Lost Productivity	F Activity Duration (Hours)	G Crew Manhours (b * f)	H Inefficient Hours (e * g)
Nov. 6	25	30	5	20%	08%	40	1200	96.00
Nov. 13	25	34	9	36%	18%	40	1360	244.80
Nov. 20	25	37	12	48%	18%	40	1480	266.40
							4040	607.20

Table 6.4. The figure at 6.5 is limited to a maximum 18 percent efficiency due to crowding. The Corps of Engineers' data is only shown for 35 percent crowding, therefore, the maximum percentage according to the Corps graph is 18 percent.

- Divide the increased crew size by the optimal crew size to determine the crowding (Table 6.4, Column D)
- Plot that percentage on the horizontal axis of the graph (See Figure 6.5). Draw a vertical line from the crowding point on the horizontal axis to the sloping line (i.e., 20 percent crowding for the week ending November 6)
- Draw a horizontal line from the intersection point on the sloping line that identifies the percentage of labor hours lost to inefficiency (i.e., 8 percent inefficiency for 20 percent crowding, see Figure 6.5)
- Multiply the percentage inefficiency loss by the new crew size and activity duration to determine the number of inefficient hours due to crowding (Table 6.4, Column H)

The total cost of inefficient man-hours on the hypothetical project due to crowding is:

Inefficient man-hours 607.20
Composite crew cost = 607.20 x $35.00 = $21,252.00

The limits of this method and the methods specified by other standards can be confusing but if accurate cost records are not kept, this method may also be acceptable for estimating losses which were actually incurred due to crowding, perhaps even after-the-fact as part of a post pricing recovery strategy.

The following is a procedure that could be used to create a post-work change order proposal:

- Define the scope of work that is changed from the base contract
- Notify the owner that you are segregating costs for change order work
- Open new accounts of record to capture the direct cost of changed work

- Create new activities and enter into the existing CPM network schedule
- Ensure that timecards are coded using the new accounts of record
- When the new work is completed, present the actual direct cost to the owner

Some of the actual costs may not have been accounted for because of impacts or consequential costs that could not be captured using the accounts of records. When post-pricing occurs, these costs are the most difficult to define and present to an owner because the effect that the changed work may have had on the unchanged base contract work is difficult to measure.

One way to capture the effect is to compare unit rates of work installed during and after performance of the changed work. It may be possible to demonstrate how the changed work made an impact on the unchanged work by comparing unit rates in the absence of changed work with those in an impacted period.

Measuring, quantifying, or estimating the effects of crowding on construction operations is not an exact science, but if the method used is not precise and the logic and reasoning are not sound, a change order or Request for Equitable Adjustment due to crowding will be questioned and perhaps rejected. To avoid this and negotiate crowding costs with factual, auditable support documentation, it is best to either:

- Negotiate the cost of labor inefficiencies due to limited work areas before proceeding on any change order; or
- Establish accurate records of crew sizes, work environments (e.g., workspace), production rates, and resulting changes in unit rate costs for installation and reserve your right for recovery of all indirect and consequential costs that result from the changes

Weather

Measuring the effects of weather on productivity can be challenging. When the seasonal shift is gradual, project teams may not be aware of the subtle but tangible changes in their productivity and won't be able to account for the increased costs and, therefore, lost profits. Simply put, not being aware of the effects of changes in weather can cost money.

Construction contracts generally have a clause addressing force majeure (the forces of nature or acts of God), such as hurricanes, floods, and other catastrophic events. Some contracts also include a clause that deals specifically with rain or other forms of precipitation. These contracts generally state that if the amount of rain exceeds a specified average (e.g., 10- or 100-year average), then the contractor(s) working on site will receive a non-compensable time extension for the excusable delay (excusable, but non-compensable).

When rain or other inclement weather inundates a project, there can be a debate about the amount of time needed for the dry-out period. The debate revolves around whether the contractor should be awarded an extension in the performance period only for the time when it was actually raining and the additional time needed to recover from the aftereffects of the rain, such as mud removal, drainage, water damage, mucking, pumping and cleaning equipment.

The costs of unanticipated changes in the weather can be both subtle and obvious. Again, removing water and mud ("muck") may take pumps, shovels, and brooms not already on site. Handling stored materials becomes more difficult, adding time needed to remove tarps and clean the materials before they are delivered to the workface.

Soil needs time to dry out. Dunnage (cribbing) and mats may have to be brought in to support lifting and heavy equipment. Bringing in fly ash to stabilize soils is an expensive and time-consuming alterative to having equipment idle and on standby. Demobilizing equipment and crews while the effects of the weather event are sorted out also takes time and costs money. Momentum is lost as crews get reacquainted with the work when the work begins again. The unit price offered in the contract may not cover the additional cost associated with changes in weather. The assumptions about costs made at bid time are not the same when there are unanticipated changes in the weather.

On occasion, because of earlier owner-caused delays, contractors may not want to seek recovery under the contract article or clause dealing with weather (rain) because the resulting delay is non-compensable. Rain can "wash away" a lot of money.

To calculate the expense of affects weather, you need:

- Awareness of the magnitude of the delays on the project as a result of the change
- To know where the project was planned to be in terms of progress on the project before the inclement weather
- A plan to get from step 1 to step 2 and calculate what it will cost

Measuring what weather does to a construction project is complex. When workers choose, or are required, to continue working in "bad" weather, productivity is affected by:

- Temporarily stopping work while the decision to cease or not cease work is being considered (show-up time)
- Causing work to be repeated because of damage by heat, frost, ice, wind, and rain
- Causing poor or reduced quality, e.g., paint applied incorrectly, concrete finishing or curing problems, steel rusting, etc.
- Reducing momentum because of starting and stopping work as a result of shortened work weeks

Costs for these types of events are associated indirectly with changes in weather and are difficult to measure accurately. Nevertheless, these costs should be considered in any request for additional compensation, be it a change order request or a Request for Equitable Adjustment or as part of a claim. Various organizations have developed methods for quantifying and measuring the effects of weather on construction productivity. These include, naming only a few:

- The U.S. Department of Housing and Urban Development, through the Center for Building Research, College of Engineering, University of Texas
- The U.S. Army Corps of Engineers at the Cold Regions Research and Engineering Laboratory, Hanover, New Hampshire

- The National Electrical Contractors Association publication, "The Effect of Temperature on Productivity," 1974

Experience and construction industry literature reviewed concludes universally there are three key weather factors that interact to reduce productivity:

- Ambient air temperature
- Wind velocity
- Relative humidity/precipitation

In 1945, the first definitive study on the relationship between temperature and wind speed was developed. The study resulted in the original "wind chill" formula shown below:

$$Te=91.4-[0.228\sqrt{V}+0.45-0.019V)(91.4-T)]$$

Where:
Te = Equivalent wind chill temperature (°F)
V = Wind speed (mph)
T = Air temperature (°F)

The National Safety Council has developed a Wind Chill Factor chart (Figure 6.6) that simplifies the quantification of the combined effect of wind and temperature. As the chart shows, consideration of the effect of wind is important in productivity-loss cost calculations because of the significant effect wind chill has on workers, craft production unit rates, and therefore, costs.

WIND SPEED MPH	ACTUAL THERMOMETER READING °F									
	50	40	30	20	10	0	-10	-20	-30	-40
0	50	40	30	20	10	0	-10	-20	-30	-40
5	48	37	27	16	6	-5	-15	-26	-36	-47
10	40	28	16	4	-9	-21	-33	-46	-58	-70
15	36	22	9	-5	-18	-36	-45	-58	-72	-85
20	32	18	4	-10	-25	-39	-53	-67	-82	-96
25	50	16	0	-15	-29	-44	-59	-74	-88	-104
30	28	13	-2	-18	-33	-48	-63	-79	-94	-109
35	27	11	-4	-20	-35	-49	-67	-82	-98	-113
40	26	10	-6	-21	-37	-53	-69	-85	-100	-116

Figure 6.6. Effective or Equivalent Temperatures in Degrees Fahrenheit (wind chill factor)

Richardson's *Industrial Estimating and Engineering Standards* indicates that, for the installation of process and mechanical equipment, the usual practice is to add one percent (1%) loss of efficiency to the cost of installation for every degree Fahrenheit below 40°F and above 85°F. If only the ambient air temperature is considered in calculating the loss in productivity, the cost calculation for lost dollars could fall short of the real effect of the cold or hot weather in which your crews will be working. Table 6.5 provides a sample calculation to illustrate the effect of just air temperature on productivity.

	A	B	C	D
	Crew	Average	(40°F-(B))	Productive
	Actual	Actual	% Lost	Lost
	Hours	Temp. (°F)	Productivity	Hours
6 Nov	652	32°F	8%	52.13
13 Nov	680	28°F	12%	81.60
20 Nov	590	26°F	14%	82.60
				216.36

Table 6.5. Temperature Effects

When the productive hours that are lost due to the temperature are multiplied by the hourly rate, the results are as shown below:

Total Crew Productivity Loss   216.36 mhr
Crew Burden Hourly Rate $ 35.00
                                     $7,572.60

When wind chill is considered and the other assumptions about how the work will be accomplished remain the same, the results are very different. Table 6.6 combines the effect of the wind and temperature in the calculations for the same hypothetical three weeks in November:

Total Crew Productivity Loss   579.70 mhr
Crew Burden Hourly Rate $35.00
                                  $20,289.50

	A	B	C	D	C	D
	Crew Actual Hours	Average Actual Temp (°F)	Average Wind Speed	Wind Chill	(40°F-(B)) % Lost Productivity	Productive Lost Hours
6 Nov	652	32°F	10mph	16	24%	156.50
13 Nov	680	28°F	15mph	9	31%	210.80
20 Nov	590	26°F	20mph	4	36%	212.40
						579.70

Table 6.6. Wind Chill and Temperature Effects

Although the temperature and wind chill comparison above did not consider relative humidity or precipitation, there is an additional $12,716 in lost productivity when the additional factor of wind chill is added to the calculation. When the effects of the wind are considered, the difference is significant.

The National Electrical Contractors Association (NECA) performed a study, The Effect of Temperature on Productivity, which considered all three factors: wind, temperature, and humidity. Figure 6.7 summarizes the findings of the NECA study. The relative humidity, expressed in percentage, is located on the left-hand vertical scale. The equivalent temperature (which includes wind chill) is shown on the bottom horizontal scale. The loss in productivity percentages can be found at the vertical and horizontal intersections of the effective temperature and relative humidity.

	56	71	82	89	93	96	98	98	96	93	84	57	0
80	57	73	84	91	95	98	100	100	98	95	87	68	15
70	59	75	86	93	97	99	100	100	99	97	90	76	30
60	60	76	87	94	98	100	100	100	100	98	93	80	57
50	61	77	88	94	98	100	100	100	100	99	94	82	60
40	62	78	88	94	98	100	100	100	100	99	94	84	63
30	62	78	88	94	98	100	100	100	100	99	93	83	62
20	62	78	88	94	98	100	100	100	100	99	93	82	61
F	(10)	0	10	20	30	40	50	60	70	80	90	100	110

Figure 6.7. Effective Temperature (including wind chill)

Although the NECA study was limited in scope, the results were consistent with other methods and studies that measure the effect of weather.

92

A study, conducted by the University of Texas on mason productivity, also included detailed research on the effects of weather. The various experiments developed for the study isolated weather as an independent variable to measure how changes in the weather affect the productivity of masons. The experiments were concerned only with the range of weather conditions in which a mason would normally work. Because building codes generally do not permit masonry construction at temperatures lower than 40°F, the study was limited to temperatures above 40°F. The study considered:

- The hourly dry-bulb temperature
- The hourly relatively humidity
- The hourly wind speed

The study resulted in a series of "productivity isopleths" and concluded that effects of weather conditions on mason productivity were "pronounced." The study also confirmed, once again, that combinations of the weather factors (i.e., temperatures, humidity, and wind velocity) have more effect on productivity than the individual elements by themselves.

The normalized productivity isopleths (Figure 6.8) demonstrates, not surprisingly, that extreme combination of temperature and humidity negatively affect mason productivity.

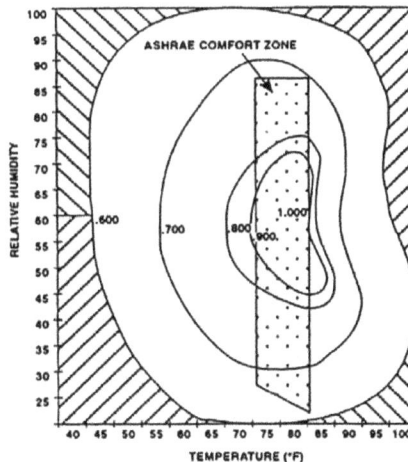

Figure 6.8. Normalized Productivity. Source: Mason Productivity Study

From the data and methods presented here, there is a direct relationship between construction productivity and certain weather conditions. Not recognizing the correlation between weather conditions and construction productivity can be very expensive and can seriously hinder progress on projects and be a major concern for owners and damage a construction firm's profitability. Weather impacts should be considered in developing construction estimates, as well as change-order proposals when delays and disruptions have shifted work into unplanned weather seasons.

Weather data can be obtained from local weather service, local airports, the Federal Aviation Administration (FAA), and from the National Oceanic and Atmosphere Administration's (NOAA) National Climatic Data Center in Ashville, North Carolina.

Construction Equipment

Owning and operating construction equipment can be very expensive. The hourly rate can range from hundreds to thousands to even tens of thousands of dollars, depending on the type and amount of equipment used. If productivity and efficiency are interfered with, the costs can quickly become extraordinary.

Construction equipment usage costs are estimated in a variety of ways, from simple per-hour rate cost estimates to detailed planning and timing of haul road routes, equipment cycle times, developing output and capacity per hour calculations based on historical data, time and motion studies, and manufacturers' data. Any combination of these methods can be used to establish an estimated production rate.

The size of the job will also dictate the equipment spread and the type of "iron" used. The estimators, equipment superintendent, and project managers determine what they believe will be the optimal mix of equipment and availability of equipment. From these variables, estimated production rates are determined.

When changes in the method of performance due to delays and disruptions and/or differing site conditions are experienced, sorting out the cost and responsibility for the potential additional cost can be a complicated task.

One way to allocate and apportion costs if delays and disruptions occur is to use the equipment production and de-rating factors provided by equipment manufacturers. Many of the job condition de-rating factors used to calculate expected production can be controlled by the construction project management team. However, some of the factors are not always within the teams' control, and when unanticipated changes occur, they can affect the cost of construction.

For instance, the Caterpillar Performance Handbook lists correction factors (Figure 6.9) that are used to modify the estimated dozing production curves also developed by Caterpillar.[2]

Figure 6.10 shows the production curves for D-10s. The equipment performance curves for other dozers were eliminated for clarity. The estimated dozing production is shown without correction factors which modify the "ideal performance" shown on the curve:

---

2   Graphs and related information Caterpillar Performance Handbook, Edition 12, Caterpillar Tractor Co., Peoria, IL

	Track-type Tractor	Wheel-type Tractor
Operator —		
Excellent	1.00	1.00
Average	0.75	0.60
Poor	0.60	0.60
Material —		
Loose stockpile	1.20	1.20
Hard to cut; frozen —		
with tilt cylinder	0.80	0.75
without tilt cylinder	0.70	—
cable controlled blade	0.60	—
Hard to drift; "dead" (dry, noncohesive material) or very sticky material	0.80	0.80
Rock, ripped or blasted	0.60 – 0.80	—
Slot Dozing	1.20	1.20
Side by Side Dozing	1.15 – 1.25	1.15 – 1.25
Visibility —		
Dust, rain, snow, fog or darkness	0.80	0.70
Job Efficiency —		
50 min/hr	0.84	0.84
40 min/hr	0.67	0.67
Direct Drive Transmission		
(01 min. fixed time)	0.80	—
Bulldozer *		
Angling (A) blade	0.50–0.75	—
Cushioned (C) blade	0.50–0.75	0.50–0.75
D5 narrow gauge	0.90	—
Light material U-blade (coal)	1.20	1.20
Blade bowl (stockpiles)	1.30	1.30
Grades — See following graph		

*Note: Angling blades and cushion blades are not considered production dozing tools. Depending on job conditions, the A-blade and C-blade will average 50–70% of straight blade production.

Figure 6.9. Job Condition Correction Factor

The correction factors shown in Figure 6.9:

- The experience of operator
- Type and condition of material being moved
- Type of dozing to be done, e.g. slow or side by side
- Job site visibility
- Job efficiency
- Type of transmission
- Type of blade
- Grade or pitch of the soil being moved

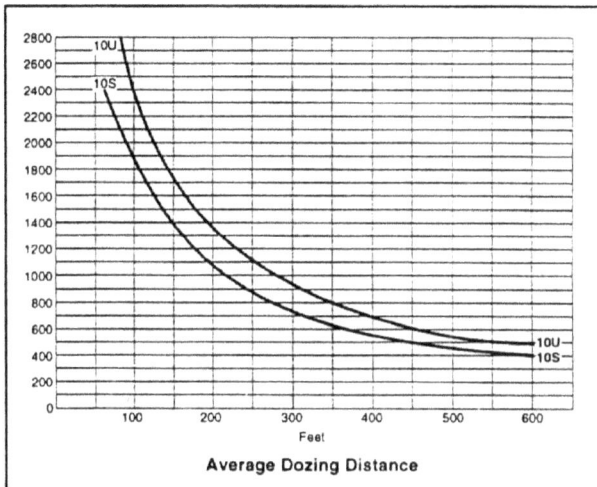

Figure 6.10. Estimating Dozing Production—Universal and Straight Blades

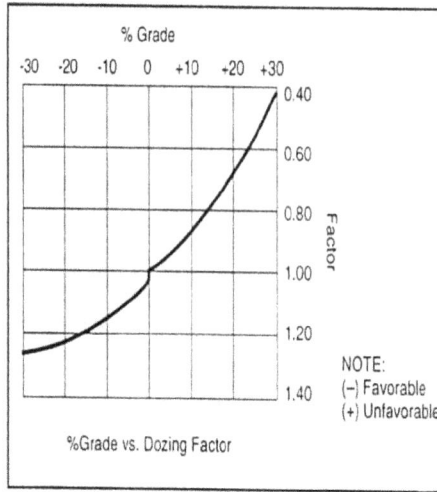

Figure 6.11. Grade Dozing Factors

It is clear that contractual issues—more specifically, delays, disruptions, or changed conditions—increase performance costs as a result of changes in job efficiency and the condition of the material being moved. The sensitivity of a production estimate to these factors and the cost of changes can be determined by the example calculations presented below.

The estimate established the average hourly production of a D-10 moving clay an average distance of 200 feet down a 15% grade in clear conditions with warm (50°f) temperatures using a slot dozing technique. It was estimated to move 150,000 LCY (loose cubic yards) at $125.00 an hour.

Job Conditions Corrections	Factors
Grade correction	1.19
Slot dozing	1.20
Average operator	0.75
Job efficiency (50 min/hr)	0.84
Soil weight correction (2300/2650)	0.87

Table 6.7. Job condition corrections

From the estimated dozing production graph for a D-10 with a universal blade (U) (Figure 6.11), the unfactored production rate is 1,300 LCY/hr. When the condition correction (derating) factors are added to the equation, the estimated production rate is reduced by 283 LCY/hr:

(1,300 LCY/hr) (1.19 grade) (1.20 slot) (.75 operator) (.84 job efficiency)

(.87 weight correction) = 1,017 LCY hr

therefore:
150,000 LYC /1,017 LCY/hr x $125/hr = $18,437 in 18 ½ workdays

However, when job conditions change (in this hypothetical case), the project is delayed into colder weather and the properties of the material are also altered by differing site conditions. The impacted production rate must be further factored by additional corrections which cause a further reduction of 498 LCY/hr. The introduction of two additional job condition correction factors (Table 6.8) and the decrease in another effectively double the cost of the project in both time and money.

Job Condition Corrections	Factors
Material (Hard to cut, frozen)	.80
Visibility (Snow, rain)	.80
Job efficiency (Reduced from .84 to .67	.67

Table 6.8. Additional job conditions

One can make the argument that the reduced job efficiency correction factor shown in Table 6.8 is redundant with the material and visibility factors and should not be included. However, other factors that are not the direct result of a change in material condition or reduced visibility may enter into the equation and lower the job efficiency. It is up to the project team to be aware of and document these events as they occur.

Most of the time, inefficiency and loss of productivity calculations are only justifiable if supported by the project records. Also, there is no substitute for tracking actual costs as they occur and associating increases in cost with changes in the project's original plan because the use of productivity factors can be challenged and their accuracy debated.

If the estimate used to bid and be awarded the job did not use the manufacturer's production rate data, contractors still should consider the job condition correction factors. Using the factors can help convince an owner or team partner of the impact of their actions in terms of dollars and time. Once it is understood that equipment production can be affected by even the slight changes, it may be easier to recover impact costs related to the actions of another party.

(1,300 LCY/ hr) (1.19) (1.20) (.75) (.87) (.80 rain, snow) (.80 hard to cut, frozen) (.67.40 min/ hr) 150,000 LCY/ 519 LCY/ hr X $125/ hr = **$36,099** in 36 work days.

Production Rate LCY/hr		$	Δ
Ideal production rate	1,300	14,423	
Correction factors anticipated	1,017	18,437	$ 4,014
Differing Site Conditions/weather impact due to delays			
	510	**$36,099**	**$17,572**

Table 6.9.Compares the ideal production rate and the anticipated production correction factors with the unanticipated correction factors that were due to unforeseen delays and disruptions.

Multiple Changes

The following describes a method used to demonstrate the costs that can occur when multiple events impact a job at the same time. Again, use a great deal of caution when attempting to use any of the industry standards to prove additional costs, the resultant inefficiency, and loss of productivity.

It is often common practice, and sometimes even an acceptable method, to use industry standards, even with their inherent shortcomings, to prove extra costs. As mentioned previously, contractors are not generally expected to, nor do they necessarily need to, keep auditable job cost reports or accounting records to support recovery of additional costs due to loss of productivity, although it is still a good idea.

One simple method of calculating the cost of various impacts is to compare a period when loss of efficiency occurred to the cost of a clean period during experiencing normal efficiency. A clean period is a benchmark of a defined amount of time that did not experience owner-caused problems where productivity was closest to the expected standard cost or control budget cost. This method is sometimes referred to as the "measured mile."

Another approach is to use the Mechanical Contractors Association of America (MCAA) Bulletin 58 to estimate damages when several separate but interrelated events impact a project, e.g. when crew sizes are increased, new work is added, site access is restricted, and an owner takes beneficial or joint (partial) occupancy all on or about the same time.

This is what's required to convert the MCAA Bulletin 58 inefficiency factors into a damage calculation. Figure 6.12 is one way to depict additional costs, which may not be segregated.

Steps:

1. Calculate the total labor hours for the impacted period.
2. Compare using the graph (Figure 6.12), the actual man-hour per month versus the planned man-hours per month. You may want to create a "conformed" estimate from the man-hours added due to approved change orders. The planned vs. actual man-hour comparison is made to show the magnitude of the variance and reinforce that the disruption was genuine. Multiply the actual hours worked by the average percentage (%) inefficiency factors.
3. Add the inefficient hours.
4. Multiply the total inefficient hours by either an hourly rate if only a single trade is involved (allowing for higher rates for superintendent and lower rates for the various

craft apprentice levels), or a composite crew hourly rate if the mix of trades is extensive or cost differences from apprentice to journeyman are significant, making the calculations too complicated.

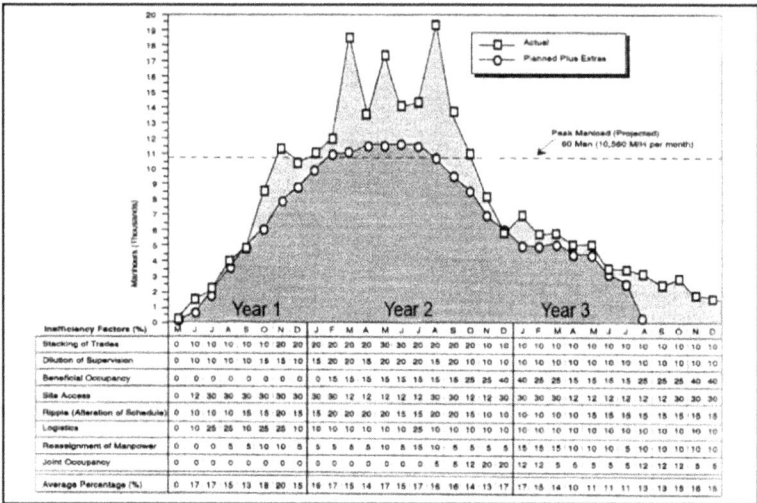

Figure 6.12. Multiple changes calculations

For example:

	A. Actual Manhours	B. (%) Loss	C. Inefficient Manhours
January	7,000	0.17	1,190
February	6,000	0.15	900
Total Inefficient Manhours			2,900
X Composite Crew Hourly Rate @ $35.50		= $74,195	

Table 6.10. Multiple changes sample calculations

The conformed estimate in this example is shown as "planned plus extras" on the graph legend.

Figure 6.12 was developed by a subcontractor who had an ongoing dispute with a general contractor. When required to produce segregated costs allocated to the disruptive events or even identify actual costs incurred, the subcontractor could not. The costs proposed, as it turns out, were a speculative estimate that could not be substantiated. The general contractor eventually paid the damages as a pass-through to the owner with significant reduction. If the general contractor, owner, and subcontractor had agreed on a method of accumulating and accounting for costs when changes to the project began, the record would have been clear and the chances of being paid for the work would have increased.

The most appropriate use for the standards referred to is in the forward pricing of changes. When changes occur, the best course of action is to follow the suggestions previously offered. Notify the owner of the potential for additional cost due to disruption. Create additional cost codes to capture direct costs. Make contemporaneous changes to the schedule to record what occurs, and record in the various project records the job conditions that are different from those that were anticipated.

Without proper precautions, inefficiency and loss of productivity costs can be very difficult to recover. Due to the federal government's complex nature of determining loss of efficiency, owners have approved inefficiency and loss of productivity change orders with relatively little evidence or explanation—but why take the chance.

A conformed estimate distributes the various cost elements (i.e., labor, material, equipment, and subcontracts) to the cost codes found in the budget created from the estimate, sometimes referred to as the standard cost. Rather than refer to the estimated cost, some contractors convert the cost estimate into a control budget, using it as the standard cost to measure and gauge progress.

Using a conformed estimate creates a more accurate picture of the change from budgeted to actual man-hours. Extra and additional costs are segregated from original contract costs, reducing confusion between contract costs and changed costs. As changes occur, the cost elements of change orders are kept separate from the contract costs, giving a more accurate picture of the actual cost of the project.

Earned Value

Various US government agencies (e.g., DOE, NASA, DOD) often require the use of the earned-value concept to manage and control their capital expenditure and procurement programs. Earned value is a method of quantitatively measuring performance to determine productivity and, just as importantly, changes in productivity.

The earned-value approach combines work packaging, organizational responsibility, work breakdown structure (WBS), a project budget, and a schedule into a management system. The earned-value methodology measures performance by computing the value of work satisfactorily completed. The amount of the earned value is calculated by periodically comparing the percentage completed for an activity to the budget and the actual cost to complete that portion of the work.

Using the earned-value concept to manage a project requires integration of budgeted cost and the project schedule. By integrating cost and schedule, three important aspects of project performance can be determined:

- Budgeted Cost of Work Scheduled (BCWS). The planned budget shows how much planned work is budgeted for completion by a certain point in time and performance milestone.
- Budgeted Cost of Work Performed (BCWP) measures the value of the BCWS completed during a specified amount of time. BCWP does not record the actual cost, but the budgeted cost (BCWS) and the percentage completed.
- Actual Cost of Work Performed (ACWP) records the actual cost to perform the work during a specific amount of time. The difference between the BCWS and the BCWP (earned value) represents the amount of time that the project is either ahead or behind schedule (schedule variance). The difference between the ACWP and the BCWP is the cost variance at a specific point in time.

The progress of the project in terms of cost and schedule can be determined by periodically reviewing the earned value and any variances that are occurring.

Again, cost variances are calculated by: $CV = (BCWP - ACWP)$
Schedule variances are determined by: $SV = (BCWP - BCWS)$

Ideally, performance is measured against intermediate or interim milestones so negative trends can be corrected and positive trends continued and rewarded. This provides a method of measuring progress and allows for:

- Mitigation of problem areas and resolution of issues
- Reward of positive trends
- Enhancement of overall management of project

There are specific formulas using the project budget, earned value, and current status information that can be used to determine productivity and efficiency. One such formula is the relationship between the budgeted and actual cost of the work, called the cost performance index (CPI). The cost performance index is determined by:

$$CPI \quad = \quad \frac{BCWP}{ACWP}$$

A similar index can be calculated for schedule performance. The schedule performance index (SPI) is determined by:

$$SPI \quad = \quad \frac{BCWP}{BCWS}$$

The results of applying these two formulas gives a ratio of planned to actual performance. It is used to gauge performance/ productivity against the original plan.

There is another important ratio formula, the budget/earned rate (B/E):

$$B/E \quad = \quad \frac{BCWP \text{ (dollars)}}{BCWP \text{ (hours)}}$$

After accounting for other sources of cost differential, such as the material quantity variance and material price variance, the labor rate variance and labor efficiency variance can be determined. Examine the potential for labor rate variances to determine if the rate being paid to the workers changes or if the composition, experience level, and crew mix changed during construction.

What remains after a review and an analysis of the labor rate variance is the labor efficiency variance. The formula below can be used to determine the labor efficiency variance (LEV):

LEV = [(BCWP hrs. – ACWP hrs.)] x (B/E rate)

How the project is performing in terms of cost and schedule can be plotted over time and displayed graphically. The trends can be visualized, and if they are negative, corrective action can be taken.

One of the most telling graphics is the depiction of the cost and schedule variances over time as shown below in Figure 6.13.

Figure 6.13 illustrates that in the first and second week of this hypothetical project, there was a negative variance in both cost and schedule. In this imaginary project, these negative variances were the result of the learning curve, when the project team was becoming familiar with the project.

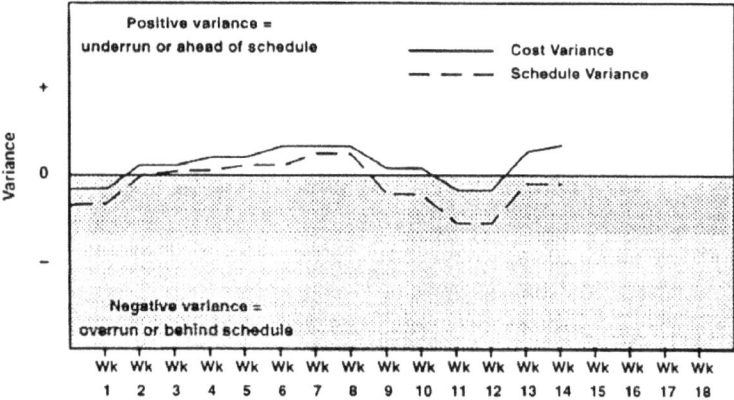

Figure 6.13. Cumulative Cost/Schedule Variance

However, beginning in the eighth week, the project was delayed and disrupted by events and circumstances beyond the control of the project team, and the project incurred losses in productivity. Note that, in this example, the delays took more time than money, as the negative variance was greater.

Figure 6.14 graphically displays the cumulative BCWS, BCWP, and ACWP of a second project. In this example, the cost and schedule are integrated, and a single graphic can be used to display

106

the general cost and schedule status of the project at any given point in time. The earned value concept also allows project teams to evaluate the progress of single or grouped accounts, allowing either a single focus or broad scope evaluation of productivity.

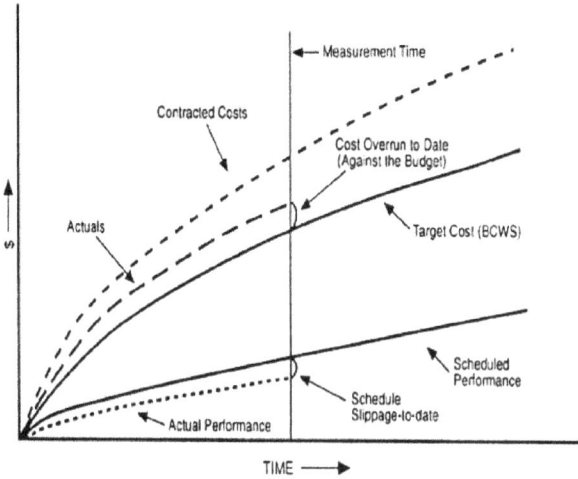

Figure 6.14. Integrated Cost Schedule System

The ability to determine earned value is a standard feature of many construction-oriented software programs for project management. Measuring productivity is an elemental and important building block of project management. Periodic productivity measurement allows for real-time adjustments to the project, performance evaluations, final cost, and profitability forecasting. Those contractors using readily available and existing software and productivity-measurement techniques can increase their profitability.

Efficiency Index Analysis and Efficiency Factors

The use of efficiency index analysis and performance factors is a way to assist with quantifying the cost of inefficiency and losses in productivity caused by the effects of changes, delays, disruptions, and acceleration.

Using efficiency factors (indices) helps quantify the effects of delays and disruptions.

Long after an initial delay, disruption, or acceleration has occurred, its presence and effects continue. The ripple of impact spreads through a job site in expanding circles like a stone thrown into calm water, affecting the entire project. Because this ripple often touches most, if not all, the project's activities, changes in productivity may be measured by an efficiency index.

Performance Factor equals:

Estimated Unit Man-hour Rate

Actual Man-hours   x In-Place Quantity Installed

Performance factors can also be calculated utilizing "Earned Quantity Installed" instead of "In-Place Quantity Installed."

The "Earned Quantity Installed" adjusts the in-place quantities for partial completion resulting in a more refined performance factor.

An efficiency index used in accounting software compares the labor costs during a period of normal productivity with the labor costs during an abnormal time period (e.g., when delays and disruptions were occurring).

For example, to develop a productivity efficiency index for normal payroll productivity, the total progress payments received for labor during an unaccelerated or nondisrupted period are divided by the total payroll costs for that same period:

Average Productivity Index (API) = TLPP divided by TPC:

Total Labor Progress Payments (TLPP)

Payroll Costs (TPC) = Total

Then, to determine what the payroll should have been during the accelerated period, divide the labor progress payment for disrupted/accelerated period by the average productivity index to give the average productivity payroll period:

Average Productivity Payroll (APP) = ALPP divided by API

Accelerate Labor Progress Payments (ALPP)

Average Productivity Index (API)

The final step is to subtract the average productivity payroll from the actual payroll. The difference is the loss of labor efficiency:

Actual Payroll (AP) - Average Productivity Payroll (APP) = Loss of Labor Efficiency (LOLE)

The disadvantage of this method is that it does not segregate additional costs and associate them with, or allocate them to, the specific issues that were the underlying causes.

If the quantification of productivity is man-hours expended per unit installed, then performance factors provide the most accurate measurement of changes in productivity. To develop performance factors, the number of actual man-hours associated with a particular cost account, divide the estimated or budgeted unit man-hour rate by the actual man-hours associated with the work. The result is multiplied by the actual in-place quantities installed.

Performance factors can be used to monitor production and forecast overall costs of the project. Trending analyses may be performed by developing performance factors and associating the fluctuating unit cost with the impacting events that occurred on the project. Trending analysis matches the facts and circumstances with performance factors to show why and how production fell below the standard/estimated rate.

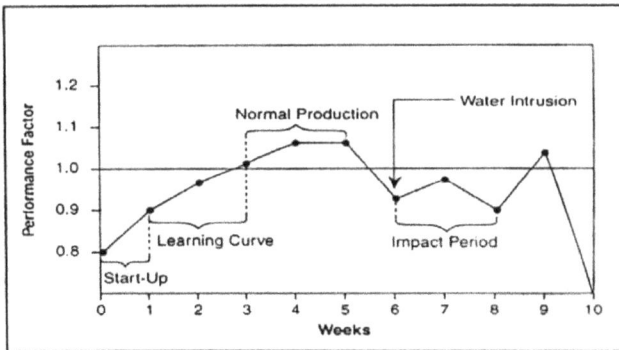

Figure 6.15. Sixteen-inch Water Pipeline Weekly Production

Figure 6.15 describes the use of performance factors to associate changes in production with project events.

In the example of the pipeline installation shown in Figure 6.15, production was below the standard (1.0) during mobilization, start-up, and the learning curve. In the third week, as the project gained momentum, productivity exceeded expectations (the standard) and that trend continued into the sixth week when groundwater began entering the excavated trenches.

Productivity declined during weeks seven and eight, as crews were required to pump water from the excavation and perform the work in generally poor conditions. The contractor did not expect water in the excavated trenches, and the estimated unit cost (standard cost) did not include the cost of removing the water. If the contractor was not contractually responsible for the water intrusion, then in this hypothetical case, the costs may be recoverable. The use of performance factors and trending analysis will help demonstrate the cause of the damage and extra costs.

Performance factors and trending analyses are useful tools for identifying potential trouble, describing changes in productivity, measuring performance, and assisting contractors in identifying extra cost and cost overruns, while demonstrating and explaining the causes for them.

Performance can be measured in terms of effectiveness or efficiency. Effectiveness relates to the completion of a specific job or achievement of an objective. A much more complex concept, efficiency relates output to input by incorporating the cost required to perform a task. The focus is on the efficiency aspects of performance rather than effectiveness.

Variance Analysis

Variance analysis is based on management by exception, where management's attention focuses on exceptions or variances from expected performance or standard.

A standard (often the budget) is a norm or criterion to judge performance. One standard for efficiency is whether a given output was accomplished within budgeted cost (input). A standard cost is a per-unit cost a company should incur to complete a unit of work.

Field managers will probably not perform variance analyses, but it's important to understand the concept so, when asked, they can contribute to the process of using it. The burden to justify additional cost to the disruptive events of the construction project is always on the contractors.

Feedback is a very important part of the cost-control process. It allows contractors to compare actual results to a budget, evaluate performance, and revise goals. By comparing actual performance with the budget and investigating reasons for variances, contractors can more accurately evaluate performance, take corrective actions, and where possible, reward employees. It also allows the contractor to revise targets and plans for future work.

Construction costs can generally be described as fixed, variable, controllable, or uncontrollable. By using standard costs and budgets, managers can develop and analyze variances for material, labor, and overhead, at either the project site or the home office. The remainder of this discussion will be limited to the variances that occur primarily at the project site: material and labor.

Actual Costs	Inputs at Standard	Budgeted or Standard
Actual Price x Actual Quantity (AP x AQ)	Standard Price x Actual Quantity (SP x AQ)	Standard Price x Actual Quantity (SP x SQ)
Price Variance:[a] (AP-SP) x AQ		Efficiency Variance:[a] SP x (AQ-SQ)

Figure 6.16. Price and efficiency variance

Construction companies calculate variances in their own unique way, based on the nature of the company and needs of its managers. However, for simplicity, we will use the fundamental variance analysis model commonly used (Figure 6.16).

The terms *price* and *efficiency variances* are general categories. Although terminology varies from company to company, the following variance titles are frequently used:

Input	Price Variance Category	Efficiency Variance Category
Direct Materials	Price (or Purchase Price) Variance	Usage or Quantity Variance
Direct Labor	Rate Variance	Efficiency Variance

To avoid unnecessary labeling, we shall refer to these variances as either *price* or *efficiency* variances.

Figure 6.17. Variance titles frequently used

Material Variance

Material price variance occurs when you purchase construction materials at a price other than the standard. Material price variance is the difference between actual price (AP) and standard price (SP), multiplied by the actual quantity (AQ) purchased:

Material price variance = (AP – SP) x AQ

This variance may result from price changes responding to:

- Market supply or demand
- Differences in quantity that changes the discounts from what was anticipated
- Purchasing (for whatever reason) materials that differ in grade from the original specifications

The accounts for variances are recorded as shown in Table 6.11.

	DR	CR
Materials Inventory (AQ x SP)	xxx	
Materials Price Variance (AP – SP) X AQ	xxx	
Accounts Payable (AQ x AP)		xxx

Table 6.11. Where DR=Debit and CR=Credit

Material quantity variance (also called material usage variance) results when actual quantity of materials used in construction differs from standard quantities anticipated. It's the difference between actual quantity of material used (AQ) and standard quantity of material allowed (SQ), multiplied by standard price (SP) per unit:

Material quantity variance = (AQ – SQ) x SP

Some potential causes for material variance:
Materials Price Variance

- Recent price changes not incorporated into the standard cost
- Substitute materials, differed from original specifications
- Change orders
- Freight cost change

Materials Quantity Variances

- Poor material handling by equipment operator
- Inferior workmanship by equipment operator
- Work required to be installed differently than anticipated
- Faulty equipment
- Excessive scrap and rework
- Inferior quality control inspection
- Base contract materials being used for change orders

For material variances, the following people should be in charge of tracking: purchasing agent or estimating department manager, project superintendent, foreman, equipment operators, material handlers.

The journal entry to record the transfer for stored material cost into work in progress inventory is shown in Table 6.12.

	DR	CR
Work in Progress Inventory (SQ x SP)	xxx	
Materials Quantity Variance (AQ - SQ) x SP	xxx	
Materials Inventory (AQ x SP)		xxx

Table 6.12. Stored materials to work in progress

Labor Variances

Direct labor variances arise when actual labor costs differ from standard labor costs. In analyzing labor costs, the emphasis is on labor rate variance: the difference between actual labor rates (AH) and standard labor rates (SH) multiplied by actual direct labor hours worked (SP):

Labor rate variance = (AH − SH) x SP

Specific causes of labor rate variances include sudden changes in overall wage rate, miscalculation of travel and subsistence payments, strikes that cause utilization of unskilled labor, and other economic or site-specific conditions that cause layoffs or uneconomical usage of skilled labor. A significant labor rate variance indicates either mismanagement of the existing labor force or changes in management decisions regarding compensation policies. Changes in actual pay rates that result from a revised labor contract or from a labor rate increase in an existing contract should be reflected immediately in a new set of standard direct labor rates for bidding new work or pricing change orders on the existing project.

114

Labor efficiency variance (also called labor usage variance), measures the relative efficiency of labor operations. If actual direct labor hours required to complete a job differ from the number of standard hours allowed, a labor efficiency variance results. The variance is the difference between actual labor hours worked and standard labor hours allowed, multiplied by the standard labor rate per hour:

Labor efficiency variance = $(AP - SP) \times AQ$

This list of variance causes is not at all inclusive, but it does contain reasons commonly used to explain why variances arise.

Labor Rate Variance

- Pay rate changes during project performance
- Employees hired at incorrect skill and experience level
- Labor strike that caused utilization of unskilled help
- Employee sickness and vacation time

Labor Efficiency Variance

- Equipment breakdown
- Inferior raw materials
- Poor supervision, lack of motivation
- Lack of timely material handling
- Poor employee performance
- Erratic production scheduling
- Defective or deficient plans and specifications
- Inappropriate crew size – too large or too small
- Concurrent operations, crowding, trade stacking
- Dilution of supervision
- Errors and omissions
- Beneficial occupancy
- Season and weather change
- Site access
- Hazardous job conditions
- New inexperienced employees
- Learning curve effects

For labor rate variances, the following people should be in charge of tracking: human resources manager, craft supervisors, and project superintendent.

For labor efficiency variances, the following people should be in charge of tracking: project superintendent, general foreman, scheduling department.

Labor rate and efficiency variances are recorded at the end of a payroll period. Once actual labor rates and actual hours are known, the following journal entry should be recorded:

	DR	CR
Work in Progress (SQ x SP)	xxx	
Labor Rate Variance (AP - SP) x AQ	xxx	
Payroll (AQ x AP)		xxx

Table 6.13. Labor rate and efficiency variance

```
DIRECT MATERIALS

$1.10 x 5,500 pounds      $1.00 x 5,500 Pounds      $1.00 x 5,000 Pounds
    = $6,050                   = $5,500                   = $5,000


        Price Variance:                Efficiency Variance:
           $550                              $500
        Unfavorable                     Unfavorable

DIRECT LABOR

$19.00 x 11,000 Hours    $20.00 x 11,000 Hours    $20.00 x 10,000 Hours
    = $209,000               = $220,000               = $200,000


        Price Variance:                Efficiency Variance:
          $11,000                          $20,000
        Unfavorable                     Unfavorable


              Total Labor Variance:
                    $9,000
                 Unfavorable
```

Figure 6.18. Cost Variance Analysis

Figure 6.18 illustrates a typical direct material variances and direct labor variances journal entry.

The following describes who on the construction team should be assigned the responsibility for recording and the reporting of standard cost variances.

Type of Variance	Personnel Responsible
Materials price variance	Purchasing agent or estimating department manager, project superintendent, foreman, equipment operators, material handlers
Labor rate variance	Human resources manager, craft supervisors, and project superintendent
Labor efficiency variance	Project superintendent, general foreman, scheduling department

Standard Cost Variance

Standard cost variance analysis is one of the more difficult jobs of cost control management. It requires considerable time to put in place, define the parameters, and update. It keeps project personnel, cost engineering, accounting department, and upper division management occupied with the analysis, but it's one of the best tools available for early detection of cost overruns, effective project management, cost control, validating cost recovery on change orders and requests for equitable adjustment, and performance evaluation.

Considering the time and cost to reconstruct variances from project records (and then perhaps to litigate a contract dispute), installing a disciplined cost accounting system that enables variance analysis to be performed as you go, makes a great deal of economic sense.

There are literally hundreds of combinations for variance on construction projects. Very often, a combination of events has contributed to the cost overrun.

Learning Curves

Learning curves are when the project team is becoming familiar with a project. Productivity is typically slower at this time, while the crews get up to speed.

Labor is one of the costliest aspects of any project. When a project is hit by delays and/or disruptions, the costs of labor soar astronomically. Learning curve analysis of productivity can be used to evaluate projects when:

- Unplanned new crews are added
- Unscheduled overtime is employed
- Work is suspended, delayed, or disrupted for an unusual period of time, and crews must relearn their work when the project resumes

Construction is a very competitive industry, and working the cost of learning curves into estimates for new work can provide the winning edge.

A comparison to an accepted standard must be made to determine inefficiency or a loss of productivity. Having a baseline of expected performance (standard costs) will enable the contractor to calculate a departure from the norm. Inefficiency or a loss in expected productivity is determined by deducting the actual cost from the expected or standard cost. The difference will include (among other things) the loss of efficiency.

The most supportable standard from which to judge variances is the project estimate or budget that generally incorporates the initial project assumptions and is typically based on historical data. To gain a competitive edge, construction estimates sometimes include productivity improvement for workers performing repetitive tasks where efficiency increases are expected due to learning. However, if delays, disruptions, or changes occur that decrease the learning curve, then the anticipated benefits and estimated production won't be realized, and the project will be less profitable than planned.

Learning curve calculations are used occasionally to justify the recovery of additional costs. For example, if a contractor is preparing loss of productivity and inefficiency cost calculations in order to present them to an owner for recovery, variances could be understated if learning curve calculations are not considered. This is particularly true if improvements in productivity due to a learning curve were a planned component of the project estimate/budget. In a change-order situation, contemporaneous documentation of the planned learning curve is crucial.

Before using a learning curve to represent what would have happened had the project not been interfered with, there must be reliable data supporting the supposition that an increase in productivity would have occurred.

There are at least five basic mathematical models for learning curves:

- Straight-line model
- The exponential model
- The Stanford "B" model
- The piece wise model
- The cubic power model

We're only going to cover the straight-line model because it is the most frequently used to represent learning curves in the construction industry. This model assumes that learning is constant each time the work experience doubles. However, this does not necessarily reflect reality as productivity improvements can accelerate in a nonlinear fashion, as experience with the task increases. To illustrate the use of straight-line learning curves to estimate productivity improvement, see the following example of a hypothetical project.

Example 6.4

A 32-floor, $68 million, architectural, concrete, office building required customized concrete forms that moved up the sides of the building by a combination of electric motors and the use of one of the three tower cranes erected on the project.

The estimator calculated that it would take 10,000 man-hours to finish the first floor.

The estimators incorporated an 80 percent learning curve, which would occur as experience was gained.

By the time the 16th floor was reached, the estimator determined that it would take only 4,096 man-hours to finish each floor.

The concrete forms would then be modified, and the next 16 floors, which have a different configuration, would be completed.

In this example, productivity improvement due to learning took place after the second, fourth, and eighth similar floors (each doubling of the work experience). The time required to produce the ninth consecutive floor was 50 percent or less than the time taken to produce the first floor. However, there is a point of diminishing return, and after that point is reached, productivity improvements level off and no further improvement is possible.

The calculations for an 80 percent learning curve for 10,000 man-hours based on this hypothetical project are found in Table 6.14.

Floor	Man-hours	x	80% Learning Curve
1	10,000	x	.80 = 8,000
2	8,000	x	.80 = 6,400
4	6,400	x	.80 = 5,120
8	4,096	x	.80 = 4,096
16	4,096		

Table 6.14. Calculations based on an 80 percent learning curve

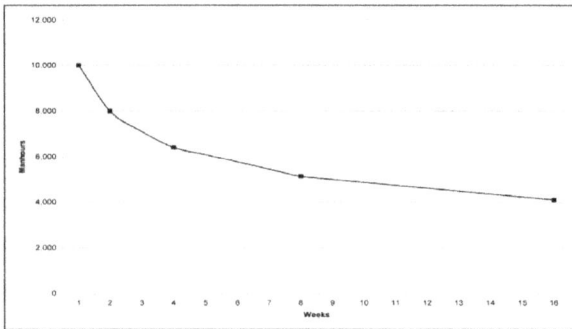

Figure 6.19. Graphically illustrates the data listed in Table 6.14.

As learning occurs, man-hours decrease significantly. When experience with repetitive tasks doubles, an additional 20 percent improvement is made each time using the straight-line learning curve calculation.

But what if significant delays and disruptions occur somewhere between the fourth and eighth floors which interrupt the learning curve? How would the lost hours be calculated and the damages accounted for? The answer can be determined by subtracting the actual man-hours from the planned man-hours for each individual floor. Can the expected productivity for the 9th through the 16th floors be used as a baseline to measure the difference between the planned and actual cost? The answer to this question is yes, because the original baseline budget had incorporated and documented a learning curve.

If the original budget did not include calculations using a learning curve, an argument to recover lost productivity may be considered suspect. However, learning curves are a genuine part of construction efficiency and productivity cost calculations. Knowledge acquired from experience with repetitive tasks is best used in estimating and bidding new work to gain a competitive edge.

When a construction company experiences trouble not of its own making, two of the most frequently asked questions are, "What will presenting a change order or claim cost?" and "What are our chances of recovery?" The answers to these questions depend on many complex, interrelated variables. There are many alternatives to consider, and each has varying degrees of uncertainty. How then, can you resolve this dilemma, provide rational, reasonable answers to these questions and make the right decision? Decision trees.

Decision Trees

Decision tree analysis is a method of problem solving by rationally examining and weighing potential options when disputed changes occur. Most issues have multiple decision paths and outcomes or there wouldn't be the need to decide; the decision is a foregone conclusion.

The goal of problem analysis using a decision tree is a solution that meets predetermined criteria and provides relative reliability and a certain comfort level for the decision. Decision tree analysis begins with a diagram (tree) of every possible outcome for the problem, with the goal of identifying the most favorable path within the tree.

The example illustrated in Figure 6.20 demonstrates the use of a decision tree. The upper branch of the decision tree represents litigation, which is an option under this hypothetical situation. The litigation option presents certain benefits, but also has its downside. The chances of recovery are good (80 percent) under certain conditions but will cost more and take longer to resolve.

The question is: should more money be invested in the litigation even if it takes longer?

Each event on the tree must be evaluated for probability and value. The probability must be evaluated using known criteria such as previous experience in a similar situation, along with an educated guess. The value of the event should consider when the payoff or result would occur. If the payoff is significantly delayed, it will be in dollars that are less valuable than if the money is received today (time value of money). The value should be reduced accordingly, using the decision tree below.

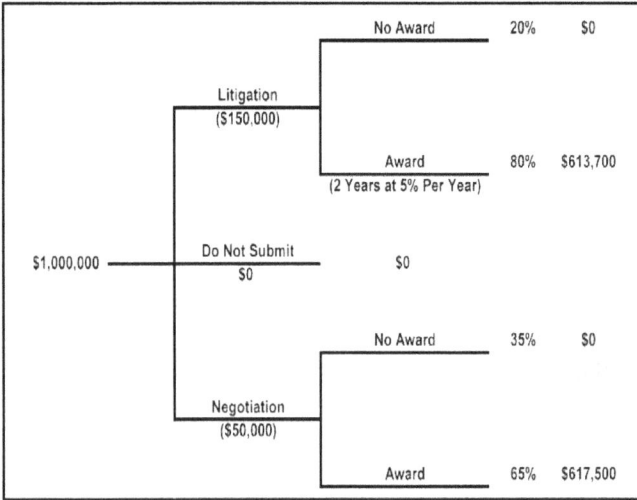

Figure 6.20. Decision tree diagram showing possible solutions and their cost and probability

In this hypothetical project, there are two acceptable paths initially. One is to litigate, and the other is to negotiate (not submitting a $1,000,000 claim is out of the question). Without performing a decision tree analysis, the prospect of an 80 percent chance of winning looks inviting. However, when the actual cost of litigation, including the interest on the borrowed money to pay the attorneys and length of time taken to get a decision are considered, then making the right choice becomes more complicated. Figure 6.20 is a decision tree diagram showing possible solutions and their cost and probability.

On another $1,000,000 troubled project, a different decision tree configuration is used, shown in Figure 6.21. Each diamond represents where decisions are necessary, the circles represent events, and the bold arrows indicate special costs.

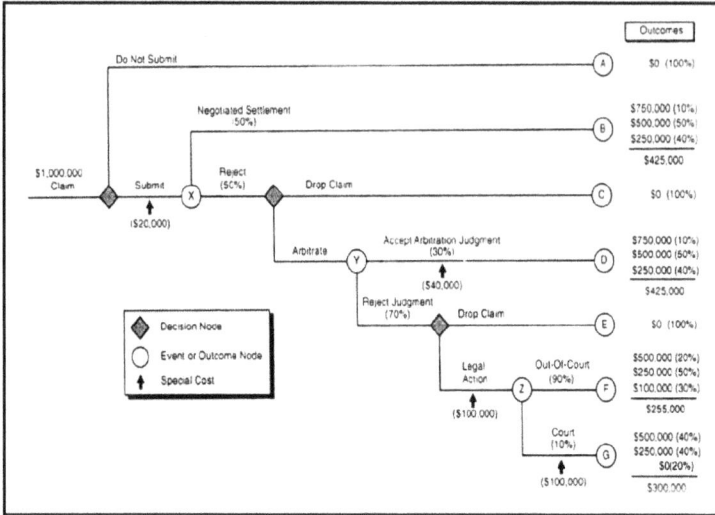

Figure 6.21. Probabilistic Decision Tree

In Figure 6.21, the outcomes (potential returns on the disputed change order) are listed in the right column. The number in parentheses are probabilities of receiving the stated outcome.

To compare the outcomes fairly, you should use a weighted average that takes into account the probability of success for a given amount.

To get the weighted average, multiply the potential dollar amount by three different percentages. In this case, 10, 50, and 40.

$750,000	x	.10	=	$75,000
$500,000	x	.50	=	$250,000
$250,000	x	.40	=	$100,000
				$425,000

Add the three potential dollar amounts together to get the weighted average.

Use the weighted averages to compare your options.

The *time value of money* and the *opportunity* or *sunk cost* should also be considered for each event. The longer it takes to resolve a dispute, the less the value of the money received.

For example, in Figure 6.21, Event X has three potential outcomes with three values and probabilities for each one. The most likely value for a settlement at Event X is the sum of the value of the three probabilities.

Decision trees are easy to create using commercially available software and can be used to explore the various alternatives before a commitment to invest additional resources is made. The decision tree method of analysis is only as good as the data and information that is associated with the branches. Without experience to rely on, the predictability of the outcome is still only a guess.

Chapter 7

Performance Measures

Establishing a standard or baseline for the measurement of performance is important at the outset of construction. Periodic measurement during construction to gauge performance and monitor progress depends on what is measured, when it's measured, and for what purpose.

Basically, it's output divided by input measured over time to understand trends and the direction of a project. Productivity measurement is at the heart of managing projects and being aware of changes. Here are various ways to define and measure productivity.

Productivity = Output/Input

Measure Output:

1. Dollar value of construction in place
2. Production units in place

Measure Input:

1. Dollar value of the resources required
2. Person-hours required to complete

Construction Productivity Measure:

Productivity =
<u>Dollar value of construction in place</u>
Dollar value of resources required

Productivity =
Production units in place
Person-hours required to complete

Productivity =
Production units in place
Dollar value of resources required

But measurement isn't always so easy. At the start of a project, bids and estimates (not always the same thing) are compiled in sometimes hectic circumstances. When subcontractors, suppliers, and vendors send in their proposals, they have various interpretations of the scope of their work and the work of the others on the job site. Each subcontractor may have conditions and reservations that it expects to include or exclude from its quote. Confusion can occur because inclusions or exclusions may be omitted, ignored or even counted twice. Management may decide to cut the bid to get the job based on the condition of the company (ie., we need the work) and market pressures. When that's done indiscriminately, there isn't an accurate way to trace the cut to a specific line item, and productivity is made difficult—if not impossible—to measure.

In the intervals between the estimate, bid award, buy out, and notice to proceed, labor materials and equipment prices can escalate or, on rare occasions, be reduced. Subcontractors may attempt to renegotiate their scope of work.

Owners can require a schedule of values for the purpose of measuring physical performance and making progress payments. A resource-loaded CPM schedule used for payment submitted by a contractor may bear little resemblance to the original bid. At this point, there may be a variety of interpretations of the planned baseline of performance. These are things used to measure the starting point for creating a baseline to measure productivity:

- The conceptual and order of magnitude estimates
- The estimate and material take off
- The bid proposal
- The schedule of values and bill of materials
- Per unit price

Failing to quantify and itemize changes at the line-item level between the estimate, bid, schedule, and budget cost control system used in accounting makes establishing losses in productivity difficult and complex. Not having reconciled the various phases can give a distorted and inaccurate picture of job performance. Job cost should not be the only measurement of performance and must not be confused with project productivity. Projects may appear to be doing well although productivity is poor.

> *Projects may appear to be doing well although productivity is poor.*

If the schedule is not periodically updated, in-place quantities not reported, labor hours not matched to cost codes, and the cost control system abandoned, then measuring productivity becomes difficult, if not impossible. The option for developing changes orders for losses in productivity is relying on trending or generalized inefficiency analysis to approximate the cost of owner-caused impacts to the job. All variance analysis depends on the reliability of a comparison of an actual versus an accurate as-planned baseline.

To have a usable baseline (standard), a reconciliation of the various phases and evolutions of the estimate is required. Once the reconciliation is made, an audit can verify that there was a rational plan and sequence of work that established the baseline for measuring performance. When changes, disruptions, or delays happen, the costs for variance between the planned performance and actual performance can be determined, evaluated, and assigned to the responsible party. The importance of having a credible, supportable baseline of planned performance for measuring productivity cannot be understated.

Performance Measurement

Again, productivity measures the difference in the rate at which work is accomplished over time, i.e. output divided by input. If you need to recover lost dollars on a project due to the owner's interference, inefficiency and loss of productivity cost calculations are easier if there is a system in place to measure job site performance. A reporting system that contemporaneously records labor usage is the most accurate and reliable method of determining the cause of inefficiency when changes are introduced or when delays and disruptions occur. However, all performance measurement methods in construction have their drawbacks and their implementation and maintenance costs.

There are a variety of methods for measuring lost time at the project site. Here are three:

- Manpower Surveys
- Timecard Notations
- Work Samplings

Manpower Surveys

The manpower survey (or delay survey) is performed daily by using a standard form (Figure 7.1) which is typically completed by foremen or superintendents. Successful survey forms list the common causes of delays that make using the form easier and promote consistent reporting. The forms may have blanks to fill in and spaces for multiplication and final numerical extensions.

The advantage of having the project field personnel make the extensions is that they get immediate feedback regarding lost time. The disadvantages are that tabulating the results takes time away from other work.

The other option is to have the contractor or a team member perform the calculations. After performing the calculations, you get an immediate feel for how time is spent on the projects for which you are responsible. After compiling the data from the surveys, the cause of lost productivity is isolated, and you can develop an educated plan to mitigate or even eliminate that cause.

The primary advantage of manpower surveys as a performance measurement tool is they take little time to implement. The primary disadvantage is that they can become routine, and if action isn't taken and visible changes aren't made, job site personnel may lose interest in the effort.

Another disadvantage is that they are tedious to analyze due to the amount of data involved. In addition, results can become subjective and biased, which could lead job site personnel to devalue the survey. Once devalued, the credibility of the manpower survey is weakened. If you take action to eliminate or, at the very least, address the causes of delays and disruptions, the manpower survey will be an effective way to segregate and associate the costs to a cause with some measure of certainty.

MANPOWER SURVEY
LOST TIME REPORT

Foreman: Bob Jones
Crew: Steel Erection Col 1-B
Date: November 3
Day: Tuesday
Weather: Cold, cloudy, some light rain p/m

DELAYS/DISRUPTIONS ENCOUNTERED

Problem		Hours	x	Men Affected	=	Man Hours
Rework:	Design Change					
	Layout Error					
	Design Error	1		3		3
	Damage					
Waiting For:	Materials					
	Tools					
	Equipment					
	Clarification	2		3		6
	Other Trades					
	Direction					
	Weather					
	Access to Work					

Comments:
Beams and Bracing didn't bolt up to columns. The drawings had a bust of 2' at L 2 elevation
100.00 Had to wait and get a fix from the structural engineer
Crane welder moved to Area C

Submitted By: Joe Brown

Figure 7.1. Manpower Survey

Timecard Notation

The timecard notation method (see Figure 7.2) uses the timecards of the individual craftsperson and allocates time to specific cost codes, recording how time was actually spent. Each timecard lists possible cost codes to use in recording how hours were spent on a particular day. The foremen record lost time for each of the workers they supervise and note the causes for lost time on the bottom of card. You can list common causes of delays on the card by number and circle or check off a lost time cost code if a corresponding delay occurs.

DAILY LABOR TIME CARD

Project: Denver Airport Project No: 9225

Date: November 15

Weather: Clear
Temperature: 68 F
Precipitation: None
Prepared By: Bob Jones

Employee Number	Employee Name	Craft	Classification	Rate	03/40 Fld Forms		03/35 Layout Ret Wall		03/35 9820		03/45 Layout Rebar	
					Hrs	Amount	Hrs	Amount	Hrs	Amount	Hrs	Amount
431	John Smith	Carpenter	J	26.50	2	53.00	3	79.50	2	53.00	1	26.50
505	Bill Stubbs	Carpenter	J	26.50	2	53.00	3	79.50	2	53.00	1	26.50
621	Wayne Lewski	Carpenter	J	26.50	2	53.00	3	79.50	2	53.00	1	26.50
Total Hours/Total Cost					6	159.00	9	238.50	6	159.00	3	79.50

Lost Time Cost Codes

Comments

The drawings had a 2' bust and the crew had to wait two hours for clarification from the A/E. Could not move to other work.

Figure 7.2. Daily Labor Time Card

Although the timecard method is the most time-consuming, it's also the most accurate method to track and accumulate the costs of changes, delays, and disruptions. Because of the paperwork effort required, there may be resistance from field personnel to the timecard method. If the foremen are made to feel threatened or believe the information collected will be used to reprimand them, the information that is reported (if it's reported at all) be skewed. However, if the data is used reasonably and rationally by management, the foremen will see that the reporting system is beneficial and meant to help them do their jobs better.

If predetermined codes are established and lost time is assigned to specific categories (e.g. defective design documents, waiting for materials, waiting for decisions on requests for clarifications, rework, etc.), a systematic, consistent, and reliable method will be in place to measure and record losses in productivity.

If the cause of the lost time originates from outside the company (e.g., the owner, architect, or subcontractor), you may show the responsible party the actual costs that resulted from their actions or inactions. Early notification of the actual costs to the responsible, and hopefully reasonable, team member(s) gives them the opportunity to rectify the situation and either mitigate or minimize costs.

Once again, the timecard method is labor intensive, but it yields an accurate picture of actual versus planned unit rates and how work hours are being spent. When the system is in place and the data compiled, the relationship between inefficiency and losses in productivity and the standard unit rates can be determined.

Work Sampling

The third method is work sampling—a statistical method used to collect information regarding the effect of lost time, productivity losses, idleness, and inefficiency. Work sampling requires trained staff to observe and record work activity on the project. Work sampling is similar to the time and motion productivity studies performed in an industrial or manufacturing setting. A trained clinical and neutral person makes random observations of work, classifying activities according to a limited preset field.

For example, an observer might record an entry similar to:

- Working-installing conduit
- Working-unloading material
- Nonworking traveling

The occasional use of video recording equipment enables observers to study the project and analyze the movements of the work force.

As observations are made, activities are generally categorized as productive or nonproductive. From the data collected, conclusions may be drawn and changes made to improve productivity and reduce lost time. Figure 7.3, depicts typical results of a work sampling study.

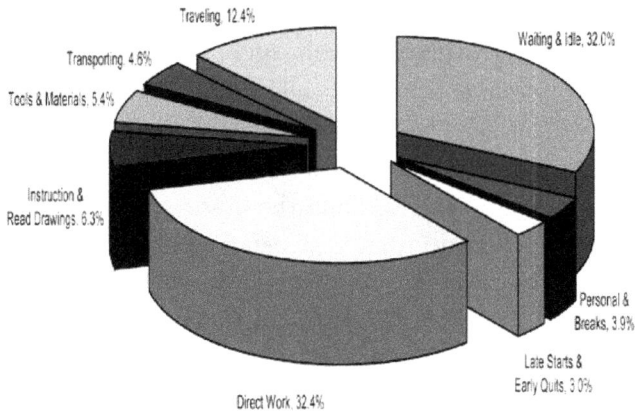

Traveling, 12.4%
Waiting & Idle, 32.0%
Transporting, 4.6%
Tools & Materials, 5.4%
Instruction &
Read Drawings, 6.3%
Personal &
Breaks, 3.9%
Late Starts &
Early Quits, 3.0%
Direct Work, 32.4%

Figure 7.3. Tpical Work Sampling Data

The flaws in work sampling as a measure of inefficiency and lost productivity are obvious: it does not measure output, nor does it explain the reason(s) for lost time. For example, work sampling tabulates that the worker was idle, waiting, or engaged in nonproductive travel but does not explain why. It establishes no real cause-and-effect relationship, only that a problem exists.

Segregating and isolating the costs of inefficiency to the actions of only one of the project team members is difficult using this method. The samples will contain only limited information relative to true job-site productivity. To draw meaningful conclusions from work sampling, you must make accurate inferences. These inferences can be highly subjective and open to argument. This is not an ideal situation when the burden of proof for the costs of changes, delays, and disruptions lies with you.

Another drawback is that craftspeople are remarkably creative and sometimes mischievous in their methods of frustrating attempts to measure or improve the status quo. If not handled correctly, they may view work sampling as a threat. If they are not made an integral part of the measurement process, they may attempt to fool observers into believing that they are productive when they are not.

There are implementation and maintenance costs involved in developing and initiating productivity reporting systems. They also require changing attitudes and habits, training, and most importantly, discipline. The benefits include improved productivity; improved project control; contemporaneous tracking and accumulating costs of changes, delays, and disruptions; and improved relationships between line and staff personnel.

Each of us may thwart needed change in our organizations, overtly or even subconsciously. If members of the workforce view changes as threatening, the effort to derail measurement will intensify. The implementation of any of the three methods of measuring productivity takes effort. The entire organization must have a stake in the outcome of measuring productivity because there is a natural resistance to change. The process must include a benefit to those personnel (usually field supervision) asked to make the effort to measure themselves. Management must recognize that there will be an adjustment period, new problems created, and new costs, but that the benefits will soon outweigh the costs of measuring productivity for whatever reason.

Disruption Costs

Disruption costs (impact and delay) can originate when an owner-caused event forces changes to the planned means, methods, order, or timing of work on a project. Disruptions have a variety of sources:

- Re-sequencing of work
- Working when conditions are unfavorable
- Having to perform unnecessary work
- Having to use inefficient methods when performing work
- Re-work

The cost of rework can be many times the initial installation cost. The work is installed. It's not right for whatever reason. It's inspected and a decision is made that it's out of specification or incompatible with the existing structure. After some debate, the decision to remove and replace or eliminate the work takes place. A new crew is asked to tear out the work. Watching their work being destroyed, the installation crew is demotivated. When the demolition starts, the surrounding work and the substrate can get damaged. New materials have to be ordered but may not be readily available. The replacement materials are transported to the workplace. The new materials are installed. The new trim and paint may not match. Then there's the time to get it inspected and finally approved.

In the meantime, the owner, inspectors, and others sharing the job site may have doubt about other work that's being done. Now the questions arise. Can the constructor be adequately compensated for having to perform re-work, and does the owner and the user group really get what they bargained for with re-work? The cost of rework may be five to six times the original cost.

Probably the most reliable way to demonstrate additional costs for disruptions is to establish account codes in the job-cost records, begin showing changes on the schedule to mirror what is happening on the project, and record the events as they occur in various project documents such as:

- Correspondence
- Meeting minutes
- Daily diaries
- Project logs

In fact, the Federal Acquisition Regulation (FAR) recognizes that contractor's accounting systems are seldom designed to segregate the costs of performing changed work, and that to be effective for cost recovery, changes to the job-cost accounting procedures may need to be made. Review the latest FAR for the most up-to-date regulation.

For example, FAR advises government contracting officers that they should tell contractors of the possible need to revise accounting procedures to comply with the cost segregation requirements set forth in the change order accounting clause outlined in FAR 52.243.6. Contractors may segregate certain categories of direct cost under the terms of the federal government's change order accounting clause for costs such as:

- The cost of reperformed or nonrecurring work
- Costs of added distinct work caused by change order
- Certain labor and material costs for recurring work

Clearly, at least in the federal arena, the government requires establishment of cost segregation and a clear audit trail. But what about payment for the increased costs of the unchanged work on the project?

As more time and attention is required for administering change orders, the cost of the unchanged base contract work can escalate. The government may impose the requirement to maintain separate change order accounts for all changes of $100,000 or more (FAR 52.243.6.). Additionally and perhaps most importantly, there is the imposition of the same requirement when the aggregate cost of a series of related changes potentially exceeds the dollar threshold. It's best to open new cost codes immediately because there's generally no control over changes and no way of knowing if or when the limit that triggers the new recommended accounting procedures will be reached.

The FAR (52.243-7) requires contractors to identify the particular cost elements, (e.g., labor equipment and materials) of contract performance to include a Request for an Equitable Adjustment. The government wants to know the particular contract line items affected by the change and what effect the change(s) will have on the schedule.

The FAR includes the additional requirement that you estimate the time the government can take to respond before delay and disruption costs begin to accrue. The point is to emphasize that both contractors and an owner should be prepared to respond to changes by altering their respective cost accounting procedures and response time as the changes begins to occur or, better yet, have the procedures in place at the outset of the project.

To avoid any confusion and perhaps hard feelings, it's better to have the conversation about handling changes at the outset of a project. In the change order estimates submitted, there is the requirement to predict and price the impact cost on the unchanged work surrounding or related to the work being changed.

Conclusion

Staying out of trouble in the construction industry is a challenge on many fronts, but it can be done. The secret is to use the contract and be able to price all the effects of changes as they occur. Calculating the inherent (often overlooked or recognized) inefficiencies and losses in productivity can be accurate when we apply common sense and good supporting documentation. It's just hard to do. It is very often part art and part science.

Done correctly, calculating inefficiencies and losses in productivity requires good recordkeeping and accurate accounting of costs. Most importantly, you should always have a clear starting point–a baseline or standard.

Project teams that define how to handle challenges up front and communicate regularly have a better chance of coming to mutually agreeable resolutions when changes do occur. Project partners that deal in good faith and support their position with facts and auditable costs invariably are more able to reach fair, reasonable settlements.

Getting started on the right foot takes time and costs money, and there are no guarantees of success. But if the right things are done initially, it will increase the likelihood of getting rewarded fairly for the work that contractors do.

Contractors significantly maximize the probability of success by setting up a budget, monitoring progress, and identifying, notifying and documenting variances, and letting everyone along the chain of command know immediately of any potential trouble. Understanding the contract and what's going on your project goes a long way to minimizing trouble. Knowing how to communicate the potential or actual cost of inefficiencies and losses in productivity will help ensure the team stays out of trouble.

Finally, we conclude where we started. Having the heart and soul of a builder has rewards found in few other occupations. The rewards include enjoyment of the work in and of itself, the satisfaction of solving problems, the positive feelings of overcoming challenges, and providing for you and your family. Actually seeing, touching, and even using a structure that you were part of creating can provide an extraordinary sense of satisfaction. A completed structure is something to point to with pride. We often hear and have said, "I built that with my own hands."

Building is an ancient and honorable profession.

Addendum

Daily Log Report

Project:

Date:

Report Prepared By:

1. Weather conditions:

    (a) Morning:

    (b) Afternoon:

2. Materials delivered to us:

3. Materials delivered to subcontractor:

4. Work:

    (a) Performed by us:

    (b) Planned by us but not performed (state the reason):

    (c) Performed by subcontractor:

    (d) Planned by others but not performed. State the reason:

5. Extra work by others authorized by us:

6. Extra work performed by us (include information concerning who authorized the extra work, description of labor and materials used to perform the extra work and whether it caused delay):

7. Accidents

8. Request for interpretation of specifications or plans (describe any inconsistencies or discrepancies, and state to whom the request is made):

9. Other comments (visitors to site and any problems encountered):

Acknowledgements

The inefficiency and loss of productivity cost calculations sections first appeared in various trade magazines as a series of articles. The author worked with some of the finest consulting firms like CRSS, FireStarter and FMI. I've enjoyed working alongside very professional contractors, attorneys, engineers, owners, and subcontractors and learned about contracts from every one of them. Thank you to the many project managers, project engineers, superintendents, and foremen I've had the pleasure of working with.

Thank you, Lenora Berg, Jennifer (Berg) Kilpatrick, and Kristen Berg, Bridger and Jones M. Kilpatrick.

References

Alfred, L. E. (1988). *Construction productivity: On-site measurement and management.* McGraw-Hill.

American Association of Cost Engineers. (n.d.). *[Institutional publication].* Morgantown, WV.

Barron's Educational Series. (2010). *Barron's law dictionary* (6th ed.). Barron's Educational Series.

CCH Inc. (1994). *Federal acquisition regulations as of January 1994.* CCH Inc.

Cibinic, J., & Nash, R. C. (1986). *Administration of government contracts* (2nd ed.). George Washington University.

College of Engineering, University of Texas at Austin. (n.d.). *Mason productivity study, Vol. III: Measurement of productivity.* (Under Contract No. H-1470 with the U.S. Department of Housing and Urban Development).

Construction Industry Institute. (n.d.). *[Institutional publication].* University of Texas at Austin.

Corbin, A., & others. (1982). *Corbin on contracts.* West Group.

Department of the Army, Office of the Chief Engineers. (1979, July). *Modification impact evaluation guide* (EP 415-1-3).

Dominiak, G. F., & Louderback, J. G. III. (1991). *Managerial accounting.* PWS-Kent Publishing Co.

Hester, W. T., Kuperus, J. A., & Change, T. C. (1991). *Construction changes and change orders: Their magnitude and impact* (Source Document 66). Construction Industry Institute.

Leonard, C. A. (1989). *The effect of change orders on productivity* (Master's thesis). Concordia University, Montreal, Quebec, Canada.

Maher, M. W., Stickney, C. P., Weil, R. L., & Davidson, S. (1991). *Managerial accounting: An introduction to concepts, methods, and uses.* Harcourt, Brace, Jovanovich.

Neil, J. M. (1992). Decision analysis using decision trees. In *Economic analysis, Cost Engineers Notebook.* American Association of Cost Engineers.

Patrascu, A. (1978). *Measuring productivity in construction: A Construction Industry Cost Effectiveness Project, Report A-1.* Craftsman Book Co.

Richardson Estimating Services. (n.d.). *Process and mechanical equipment installation, Industrial estimating and engineering standard* (Vol. 1, Account 8-1, p. 1).

Sharad, D. (n.d.). *About delays, overruns & corrective actions.* Project Management Institute.

Siple, P. A., & Passel, C. F. (1945). Measurements of dry atmospheric cooling in subfreezing temperatures. *Proceedings of the American Philosophical Society, 89,* 177–199. (Cited in Abele, G.)

Sweet, J. (1977). *Legal aspects of architecture and the construction process* (2nd ed.). West Publishing Co.

Thomas, H. R. (1992). Effects of scheduled overtime on labor productivity. *Journal of Construction Engineering and Management, 118*(1), March.

Thomas, H. R., et al. (1986). Learning curve models of construction productivity. *Journal of Construction Engineering and Management, 112*(2), 245.

Thomas, H. R., Jr., & Matthews, C. T. (1986). *An analysis of the methods for measuring construction productivity* (Source Document 13). Construction Industry Institute.

U.S. Army Cold Regions Research and Engineering Laboratories. (n.d.). *Effect of cold weather on productivity.* Hanover, NH.

U.S. Army Corps of Engineers Construction Research Laboratory. (n.d.). *[Institutional publication].* Champaign, IL.

Uniform Law Commission. (n.d.). *Uniform Commercial Code.* https://www.uniformlaws.org/acts/ucc

www.ingramcontent.com/pod-product-compliance
Lightning Source LLC
Chambersburg PA
CBHW071701210326
41597CB00017B/2271